CW00558382

"*Changing Lives* is easy to read, covers all the key
and is full of great stories and wise advice. But t
this book essential reading is that Mark not o
ministry is vital, but leaves you believing that it is possible. Great theology made
practical, based on solid research, wrapped in infectious optimism."

**Revd Professor Jeremy Duff, Principal of St Padarn's Institute,
Church in Wales**

"*Changing Lives* is a wonderfully reflective and practical book underpinned by
useful theology, rich experience and superb storytelling. Mark's reflections on his
journey as a practitioner in Children & Family Ministry include much wisdom
gained from his experience and studies making this book accessible and a 'must
read' if you're new to ministry or have been at it a while and need to reflect and
refocus. 'What else can God do?' is an important question asked in this book and
one every practitioner should be seeking the answer to in their own context. Great
stuff, thanks Mark!"

Yvonne Morris, Oxford Diocesan Children's Advisor

"Packed full of great stories, godly wisdom and good advice. This is a goldmine
of tested resources for people who know the Father's big heart for small people"

Paul Harcourt, National Leader of New Wine England

"This book is about ministry in four dimensions... the key one of which is the
fourth... that says, 'Go and do it!' For this reason alone I commend this book. It
is written by a practitioner in children's ministry calling on others to get involved
in a way that includes the insights of children."

**Revd Dr Howard J Worsley, Vice-Principal & Tutor in
Missiology at Trinity College Bristol**

"This book shouldn't be read by anyone hoping for a nice affirmation of the
status quo in relation to the church's ministry to the family, young people and
children. In this pithy and persuasive book, Mark challenges us to be real about
our priorities. He mixes an analysis of data with a sharp understanding of social
media and a more discerning society than is often acknowledged to show we need
not been despairing but rather re-oriented towards those who long for values and
a way of belonging that should be at the heart of our mission. I'm delighted to
commend this book."

Rt Revd Andy John, Bishop of Bangor

Other books by Mark Griffiths:
Fusion
Impact
Detonate
Hanging on Every Word
One Generation from Extinction

CHANGING LIVES

THE ESSENTIAL GUIDE TO MINISTRY WITH CHILDREN AND FAMILIES

MARK GRIFFITHS

MONARCH
BOOKS

Published by Monarch Books, an imprint of
Lion Hudson Limited
Wilkinson House, Jordan Hill Business Park
Banbury Road, Oxford OX2 8DR, England
Email: monarch@lionhudson.com
www.lionhudson.com/monarch

ISBN 978 0 85721 825 4
e-ISBN 978 0 85721 826 1

First edition 2003

Acknowledgments

**Every effort has been made to trace and
contact copyright holders for material
used in this book. We apologize for any
inadvertent omissions or errors.**
Illustrations: ElenaMedvedeva/iStockphoto;
Colouring sheet: ya_mayka/iStockphoto;
Invitation: Nadzeya_Dzivakova/iStockphoto
Unless otherwise noted, Scripture
quotations are from the Contemporary
English Version New Testament © 1991,
1992, 1995 by American Bible Society, Used
with permission.
Scripture quotations marked ESV are from
The Holy Bible, English Standard Version®
(ESV®) copyright © 2001 by Crossway,
a publishing ministry of Good News
Publishers. All rights reserved.
Extracts marked KJV are from The
Authorized (King James) Version. Rights
in the Authorized Version are vested in the
Crown. Reproduced by permission of the
Crown's patentee, Cambridge University
Press.
Scripture quotations marked NIV are taken
from the Holy Bible, New International
Version, copyright © 1973, 1978, 1984
International Bible Society. Used by
permission of Hodder & Stoughton, a
member of the Hodder Headline Group.
All rights reserved. 'NIV' is a trademark of
International Bible Society. UK trademark
number 1448790.
Scripture marked NKJV is taken from the
New King James Version. Copyright © 1982
by Thomas Nelson, Inc. Used by permission.
All right reserved.
Scripture quotations marked NLT are
taken from the Holy Bible, New Living
Translation, copyright © 1996, 2004, 2007
by Tyndale House Foundation. Used by
permission of Tyndale House Publishers,
Inc., Carol Stream, Illinois 60188. All rights
reserved.
Scripture quotations marked NRSV are
from The New Revised Standard Version of
the Bible copyright © 1989 by the Division
of Christian Education of the National
Council of Churches in the USA. Used by
permission. All Rights Reserved.
Scripture quotations marked RSV are from
The Revised Standard Version of the Bible
copyright © 1346, 1952 and 1971 by the
Division of Christian Education of the
National Council of Churches in the USA.
Used by permission. All Rights Reserved.
Scripture marked The Message is taken
from The Message. Copyright © by Eugene
H. Peterson 1993, 1994, 1995, 1996, 2000,
2001, 2002.
p. 112: Lyrics from "Lovely Jubbly" by Doug
Horley © 2001, Doug Horley. Reprinted by
permission of Thankyou Music admin by
Integrity Music.
pp. 112–13: Lyrics from "Be Happy"
by Doug Horley © 2001, Doug Horley.
Reprinted by permission of Thankyou Music
admin by Integrity Music.
p. 145: Lyrics from "God Put a Fighter in
Me" by Graham Kendrick © 1978, Graham
Kendrick. Reprinted by permission of Make
Way Music.
p. 169: Extract taken from Absolute Truths
by Susan Howatch © 1996, Susan Howatch.
Reprinted by permissions of HarperCollins
Publishers Ltd.

A catalogue record for this book is available
from the British Library

Printed and bound in the UK,
February 2018, LH26.

This book is dedicated to my wonderful wife, Rhian,
and my fabulous children Nia, Owen and Elliot. I love you,
and continue to be so proud of the way that
you are growing in God.

"A four-year-old prayed for her mum's back and saw her healed."

(April Hammond, Kerith Community Church, Bracknell, Berkshire)

"We have a boy in our kids' club who, due to anxiety, is selectively mute. Tonight we asked the children to say their names and something they like, out loud, for a new child and leader. I was standing by to speak for the boy if he needed that but he boldly spoke for himself! In front of the whole group! I'm so chuffed he feels safe enough to speak with us."

(Yvonne Morris, Oxford Diocesan Children's Advisor)

"In our children's group it has now become normal that children minister to each other."

(Alex Scott, Holy Trinity Leicester)

"Our son had an amazing time, signing all the songs without any assistance. Thank you doesn't seem enough."

(Naomi Graham, King's Cross Church – mum of a son who has additional needs recorded.)

Miracles happen all the time.

Contents

Acknowledgments

A big thank you to Rachel Hill-Brown, Alison Champness, Jo Foster and Lisa Macbeth, who have all contributed chapters to this book. You'll see very quickly how brilliant their contributions are.

And also a thank you to Mike Archer, Jenny Bentley, Jackie Faerber, Jo Foster, Hannah Jenkinson, Victoria Jones, Lucy Vitale, Howard Worsley, the Northumbria Community, and so many others who were my rocks in 2016.

And of course to the thousands of children and children's workers whose lives I have had the privilege of being involved in, and to those dazzling teams, now being led by the amazing Rick Otto, who made New Wine such a fun thing to be part of. You change the world on a daily basis. Sometimes before breakfast.

Thank you...
And a special thank you to Simba Bhebhe, Laura Conway, Sean Harriott, Simon Hicken and Jonathan Logan with whom I started Frantic in the early 1990s at Milton Keynes Christian Centre – my first experiment with a mega children's outreach project. And to Grant Smith, Chloe Shrimpton and the team at St Mary's Bletchley, with whom we launched Dream Factory – by then I'd got the hang of it! And to Jo Foster, Jackie Faerber, Debs Fenton (now working with Bill Wilson and Metro World Child), Nia Griffiths, Owen Griffiths, Sam Holloway and Scilla Summers, with whom we launched All Starz in my time as senior minister in Bracknell in Berkshire. Over three decades of ministry to children and families – what a privilege. All three outreach projects continue to touch the lives of children and families today – long may they continue!

Foreword by Bill Wilson

As founder and senior pastor of Metro World Child, I've been in full-time ministry for over fifty years and I've seen and heard pretty much everything. There are so many books out there today that are all trying to do the same thing – they either tell you how to do something or how not to do something. Half the time they're written by people who haven't done anything!

Mark Griffiths goes against the grain with this book by covering key components of ministry; he has created exactly what's in the title: an *essential* guide for those who are interested in, or who are already involved in, children's ministry. Over the course of reading this book, you'll understand how critical it is to reach boys and girls *before* they become men and women, with the purpose of prevention versus intervention. This concept is the foundation of reaching children, whether it's in your church, your town, or the other side of the world.

Changing Lives allows the reader to gain spiritual and practical knowledge to bring a relevant, real gospel to the lives of others. And folks, you'll soon realize that all it takes is someone with an open heart, an open mind, and the belief in a God who can do just that – change lives. And the best part of it is – that someone is YOU! Be available, be ready, and allow God to speak to you through the pages of this *Essential Guide to Ministry with Children and Families*.

Bill Wilson (Founder and senior pastor of Metro World Child)

A Word from the Author

Originally this book was called *The Definitive Guide*.[1] It is the successor to the 2003 book *Don't Tell Cute Stories – Change Lives!*, which has the strapline "The can-do guide". Surely by now I'd reached "definitive"? Nevertheless, when I reached the end, I was convinced that there would always be more to write about and a decade from now I will undoubtedly be knocking on the publisher's door suggesting an update. Therefore, we changed it to *The Essential Guide*. And I believe that. The title has integrity. There are principles and practices within this book that are *essential* to developing significant ministries to children and families.

It's likely that you are not going to read it cover to cover – hopefully many will – but for some, you'll dip in and out as the need arises. Because of that an overview of the overall structure of this book will help:

Introductory chapters, as you might expect deal with the reason you should read the book. It is intended to touch your heart. The following initial chapters then present the context in which ministry happens today. All theology is practical theology (it has to work in practice) and all ministry is contextual (it happens in a specific place at a specific time).

Section 1 looks at children's ministry in four dimensions. Three dimensions looking at the biblical basis for our work with children and families specifically:

- **Dimension 1:** Our immediate family
- **Dimension 2:** Our extended family/church community

---

1   I made the mistake of asking others, on Facebook, for an opinion on the title. I was desperate to include all responses, but when I copied them all and reduced the font size to 10 it still ran to seventeen pages of A4!

- **Dimension 3:** The unchurched, i.e., the communication of the Jesus story to boys and girls who wouldn't hear that story in any other way.

And finally:

- **Dimension 4:** Outlines the most important factor, which is of course YOU.

Section 2 examines the important part that communication plays. The person who learns to communicate to a generation can influence that generation. This section also dips into the theological underpinning; what we communicate.

Section 3 deals with the need to expose a few "sacred cows".

Section 4 builds on the first two sections and adds practical help. All theology is practical theology. If it doesn't actually work, then it's not good theology.

And the book concludes with some "Extra Stuff", for example, sample schools contact letters and finally some recommended resources.

This book is "essential", yes. But not difficult. If a person with the right heart takes hold of it and applies what is found here then I dare to believe you will significantly impact the lives of children and families throughout our world and will join with the rest of us in the task of the re-evangelization of our community, country and world.

Revd Dr Mark Griffiths (June 2017)

This is What it is All About

It was my final year in theological college, I was twenty-two. And like many other students I had been wondering what the future would hold. It was a cold night and the rain hadn't stopped for several days. By now it was approaching midnight and I was lying in my bed, I found the rain hammering against the window comforting. I was beginning to drift off to sleep when I felt God speak. I had been a Christian for only six years, and had spent the last three in college, but I knew when God was saying something.

"Do you really care about the young people and children of this nation?"

"God, you know that I do," I instantly responded.

The conversation continued, "If you really care then I want you to pray now."

I rolled out of the quilt and knelt beside my bed. I began to pray when God prompted once again.

"If you pray there you will be asleep."

I know that God knows all things, but I don't think He was particularly stretched in that revelation. I pulled on my clothes and suggested to God that we could probably do this tomorrow if He wasn't too busy. Still, I ventured out into the wet night and made my way to one of my favourite prayer spots, a footpath bridge that crossed over a river. It took me less than ten minutes to get there, but by the time I arrived I was very wet. There was certainly no chance of dropping off to sleep, but I also didn't much feel like praying – I was wet and cold. The rain was hammering down and the river looking particularly rough. The only prayer I was praying was "God, what am I doing standing here?" There was no response.

I stood for a little longer and was about to make my way back when I saw two other students walking towards me. Contrary to urban myth it is not commonplace for theological students to be walking around at midnight in the rain, let alone to find three of them out at the same time. They approached me and asked, "Did you hear a scream?"

I shook my head. I hadn't heard anything except the wind and the river. We concluded that it must have been someone having a nightmare back at the college. They asked if I was OK and when I nodded they made their way back to college. I stood a little longer and was about to make my way back when God spoke again. This time more clearly than I had ever heard him before, or since. He said, "The sound that I hear is a constant scream, the scream as millions of children are aborted before they are born, the scream as they are hurt and abused, the scream as they feel helpless and nobody cares, the scream as they feel lost and alone and carry those scars into their adult lives, the scream as relationship after relationship lets them down and the ultimate scream as they topple helpless and alone towards hell."

By now I was wet through to the skin, I was shivering with the cold and if anything the rain was coming down faster and the wind blowing more ferociously. But I didn't care about the wind or the rain, I had felt something that God feels: I had shared for a *microsecond* an inkling of the pain that Father God *feels*, and for a brief moment I understood how desperate God was to reach these children.

"God," I prayed. "I want to make a difference. Use me to reach these children, to connect with these families. God use me."

I prayed and kept on praying. The rain continued to fall, the wind continued to blow and I continued to pray. Into the night I prayed... Amy Carmichael was a missionary in the nineteenth century. One night she had a dream. In her dream she found herself on the edge of a cliff. Far below she could see the waves hammering onto the rocks. And as she stood there she saw people rushing towards the edge of the cliff. She ran back and forth trying to stop them falling off the cliff. She managed to rescue many but she couldn't get to them all.

Then she noticed that not far from the cliff's edge there were people sitting on picnic blankets making daisy chains. In her dream Amy shouted to them to come and help, but they didn't move, they continued making daisy chains. Amy continued running back and forth rescuing those she could.

And then she woke up. She asked God what it meant. God explained that she was rescuing the people who were walking and toppling over the cliff towards hell. Those who sat and made daisy chains represented the church of her day, wrapped up in complacency, apathy and indifference.

I do not believe that the church today is the same as the church in Amy's day. I genuinely believe that for the most part we have conquered the enemies of indifference, apathy and complacency. But we are now facing an even more subtle enemy. Our biggest enemy today is not indifference or complacency or apathy; it is not inactivity – it is instead activity! We are all busy doing something. We all seem to be engaged in frenetic activity. Our lives becoming increasingly busy. And our churches are not immune. Huge activity dedicated to "helping people". But what we have inadvertently done is this: instead of standing on the edge of a cliff we have opened a range of rescue services at the foot of it. We wait until people fall off the cliffs and onto the rocks below and then we try and help them. We wait until their lives are in pieces and then we offer to put them back together. We are trying to perfect the art of repairing men and women. In the twenty-first century the church has some of the best counselling services available. We can counsel drug addicts, we can counsel alcoholics, we can counsel those who are having relationship problems, we can counsel those who were bullied at school... pick a problem and we have a counselling service for it! Lots and lots of activity, lots of people working furiously at the bottom of the cliff but very few at the top. My grandmother put it this way, "Prevention is always better than cure."

Children's ministry stands at the top of the cliff with arms open wide. **It is about building strong children, making them secure, introducing them to a God who loves them.** Showing them a godly example and convincing them that they have a destiny that God set apart for them even before He began to put the universe together. The Bible leaves us in no doubt that the devil comes to kill, steal and destroy. To kill innocence, to steal destiny and to destroy lives. It is sheer stupidity to watch as the devil does these things and then some years later try and repair the damage. We must reach children before they hit the rocks. We must stand at the edge of the cliff. The tragedy is that 80 per cent of the church's resources are still being poured into repairing men and women. We must work to change this, but as we work we must stand at the edge of the cliff.

I have a vision. A vision of children and family workers across our entire world with linked hands, committed to winning a generation for Jesus. Committed to the re-evangelization of their community, their country and their world. It is possible.

Our churches glamorize and sensationalize the man or woman whose life was in ruins on the rock and then was put back together. Those who were drug addicts, murderers, thieves and muggers pack our arenas as they tell how God changed their lives and I cheer with everyone else, I stand in awe at the grace of God, but I take great exception at those who then mutter, "Wasn't that a great testimony?" The answer is "no". That was not a great testimony. It was great to see God changing a life, it was great to see the Holy Spirit drawing a sinner back to Christ, but it is not a great testimony. Great testimonies are those where a person stands and tells of how they gave their life to Jesus at a very young age and they felt God speaking to them and they lived their life for Him and they became a doctor, or engineer, or miner, or missionary and served God all their lives – now that's a great testimony. It's not so dramatic, it may never pack arenas, but never let go of the fact that this is what we should be aiming for.

I am not advocating that we close our counselling centres: there will always be those that slip through and better that we reach them later on than that we don't reach them at all. But, at the same time let's keep the ultimate aim in our minds. Reaching boys and girls. Right now:

- 39 per cent of churches have *no one* attending under eleven;
- 49 per cent of churches have *no one* attending aged eleven to fourteen;
- 59 per cent of churches have *no one* attending aged fifteen to nineteen.

It's time to hear that scream for ourselves and take our place on the edge of that cliff.

The Eighteenth Century Was Drawing to a Close

One Sunday in 1780, a Gloucester businessman looked out of the window of his workshop and wondered why there were so many children not in church.[2] He embarked on what he was to term his "strange experiment".

He embarked on it not because the booming voice of the Lord spoke to him. Not because of a prophetic word or inspired passage of Scripture. No burning bushes (which when your business is producing newspapers must be something of a relief); just a man who looked out the window and saw a need.

Let's look out of the window. Let's recognize the need. It may be on our doorstep; it may be nationally perceived or it may be an international disaster leaving tens of thousands of refugees without homes. Sometimes the need is the call.

This particular Gloucester businessman was Robert Raikes. What he was about to create was the first children's ministry. We know it today as the "Sunday School Movement". Within eight years 300,000 children from primarily unchurched homes were connected to church and church groups in England alone. By 1830 the adult population of the church in Britain would double in size, certainly in part due to children growing up and becoming adult members in the churches that had reached out and nurtured them. John Wesley gave explicit instructions that if a new church building were to be built it should be built on two levels: the lower levels for the Sunday school and the upper for family church. Wesley stated that it should be the expectation that children graduate Sunday school (usually at the age of fourteen in those days)

---

2   Yes, you did read that correctly. This incredible institution that would see 85 per cent of the child population of the UK in church or attached to church groups by 1900 was built on hypocrisy! Robert Raikes was working on a Sunday to finish his newspaper and he asks, "Why are those children not in church?" God really will use anyone who makes themselves available to him.

and take their regular place with the rest of the congregation.

Successful ministry to children and young families enables churches to grow. The lack of it means decline. In many parts of the world there are now more salaried children and family workers than there are salaried youth workers. Why? Because the church has recognized that early intervention is **the** key to transforming the church and ultimately changing the world. But we're not there yet. While churches are increasingly recognizing that ministry to children and young families is essential to their future, they are yet to fully grasp **how** to do this effectively and overall they are still not certain **what** a successful children's and family ministry would look like.

I have been involved in this vital ministry area for over three decades: as a volunteer in the children's ministry, as a salaried children and family pastor, as a lecturer in many of our theological colleges, as a seminar and workshop speaker at many conferences, as the associate minister with oversight of children and families – and for much of the last decade, as senior minister. I have ministered in most denominations and in a lot of different countries. I have learned some important keys in each of those roles. I know that when churches are left to their own devices they become cliquey, get older and eventually decline. I know that the job of leadership is to ensure those things don't happen. I also know that all healthy churches grow. And health means major investment in children, young people and young families.

Over three decades I have learned that our ministry to children and families can be exceptional if time and energy is given to just four primary areas – the four dimensions of children and family's ministry. This book looks at those four dimensions. But before we go there. Let's pause and consider what we are dealing with as we have well and truly entered the twenty-first century.

A Brave New World

Ministering in a Postmodern Culture is Not as New as You May Think

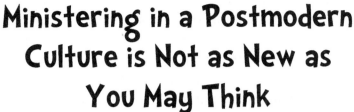

My youngest son started secondary school a few years ago (I am not at all sure how they all got so old; when I wrote the first edition of this book my eldest child was about to start primary school!). The thought of going to "big school" was causing him some concern. Not in a small way because his brother (my middle child) had convinced him that every new arrival in "big school" had to go through something called "swirlies". It seems the traditions continue from generation to generation but we simply change the names. "Swirlies" meant that the big boys would be dipping his head in the toilet and pulling the chain in his first week. I assured him that this wouldn't happen. But he believed his big brother because he was at the school already... despite my mentioning his brother's reputation for telling him all sorts of made-up stories.

Then he started his new school. And at the end of the first week he came to find me because he was feeling upset. "Swirlies" hadn't happened and he wanted to know if the big boys didn't like him? He'd concluded that all the other boys must have had "swirlies" done to them and he hadn't! Secondary school was a strange world. A new culture. Nothing felt the same as the safe single classroom or the single teacher of primary school. For the first few months he carried around every text book he'd been given in case he missed a subject. His bag was beyond heavy. He was adapting to a new culture. A new way of operating. But curiously, he had stumbled on the key to engaging with any new culture. Even this brave new twenty-first-century world.

The apostle Paul had gone through a similar process in his missionary journeys. He'd arrived in Corinth and it was very clear that there were already a range of factors at play: sociological, economic, religious. Corinth was a combination of numerous cultures that had come together to form a new hybrid culture. It was a mixture of rich and poor. Merchants making their wealth through relatively newly opened trade routes, freedmen (freed slaves) who had left Rome and were industrious in carving out a living. Rome was of course dominant, but Rome itself was a sponge in terms of culture, soaking up everything it encountered and making it part of itself. Therefore Corinth was home to Roman and Greek gods, "mystery" religions that had migrated from the East and of course Jewish synagogues as the Jewish nation began to spread out. Temples emerged to numerous gods. And the people of Corinth had no issue with engaging with whichever deity they felt could give them a response in their present circumstances. When Paul entered Corinth it had twenty-six different temples. So what do you do? A new world to engage with. Where do you begin? Let's see if we can find a few keys.

Firstly, we must understand the mission – it's straightforward enough. Go into all the world and preach the gospel, baptize them and help them become mature followers of Jesus.

Secondly, don't fall into the trap of thinking people are not spiritual. They are hugely spiritual. G. K. Chesterton said that when we stop believing in God we don't believe in nothing, we begin to believe in everything. James Fowler wrote a book called *Stages of Faith*. It needs careful critique, but what he gets right again and again is that people are still spiritual. One of his interview candidates was four-and-a-half-year-old Sally. Sally had been kept away from all forms of organized religion by her parents. But yet under interview she still had a deeply spiritual view of the world and understanding of God. Thirty years in children's ministry in a variety of countries has taught me this clearly: **all children are deeply spiritual and want to connect with God.**

But how do you do that in a foreign culture? Paul knew the pattern for Jews. There was much in common. Monotheistic religion (one God), the same moral code (based on the Torah and ten commandments) and an easily identifiable place of worship – the synagogue. And of course Paul was a very well educated Jew. He entered the synagogue and presented his argument explaining that Jesus was the fulfilment of the Old Testament law. And that has worked for us for a while by the way. For many centuries the UK had a residual understanding of

Christianity that you and I could work with. People visited churches, vicars and ministers were commonplace. But not so in the years of decline in the twenty-first century where there are now some homes where four or five generations in some families have never been to church. That alongside the influx of other religions and belief systems.

So what do you do? Children and families don't readily wander in to the church. Let me firstly point out something interesting. Paul is trying to work it out too. We think he's got it all together. We think he is the super evangelist. Weeks before walking into Corinth he has stood in Athens and, seeing the inscription "to the unknown god", starts where the people are at and preaches from there. He is trying to work it out and, as a result, a few people become followers of Jesus. Not Pentecost. But not a bad first attempt. But it gives us our first clue as to what you have to do in an unknown culture. You have to get experimental. It's the Robert Raikes pattern from the last chapter. We simply don't know what will work so we have to try lots and lots of different things. Some will work and some will fail and you will see this statement a few times in this book: **Failure is completely overrated.**

So when Paul arrives in Corinth he has solution number one pinned down: **You must experiment.**

It has been this way for centuries. Kenyan philosopher John Mbiti says that, "Christianity is always the beggar at the door looking how it might present itself to each new culture."[3] The wristbands stating "WWJD" are exactly the response. No blueprint, but the application of revealed truth into the new situation we face. What would Jesus do?

But Paul also learns a few new things to add to that. In Corinth he doesn't arrive, preach and leave. He arrives, sets up home among them and begins to learn their culture. He immerses himself in their world. Not the knight in shining armour who rides in, saves the damsel and departs. That doesn't work.

This is the incarnational ministry of Jesus. He comes and lives there.

When you live there, all sorts of things change and, fundamentally, the way that we communicate. There is a radical change in Paul. Paul is didactic; he likes systematic, logical presentation of truth. He is big on

---

3   Mbiti, J. "Christianity and Traditional Religions in Africa", *International Review of Mission*, Geneva: WCC Publications, 1970.

cognition; he preaches to the mind. But in Corinth all those principles go out of the window. Here it is in 1 Corinthians 2:6–8 (NRSV):

> Yet among the mature we do speak wisdom, though it is not a wisdom of this age or of the rulers of this age, who are doomed to perish. But we speak God's wisdom, secret and hidden, which God decreed before the ages for our glory. None of the rulers of this age understood this; for if they had, they would not have crucified the Lord of glory.

The inhabitants of the first-century Greek world liked to talk. They liked information. They liked to communicate information. In fact, they would have been really at home in our information-based world of the last fifty years. Our news services are almost instantaneous. You can Google™ anything! When I typed in Corinthians to Google it gave 18 million hits in 0.43 seconds. And that information is accessible all the time because we walk around with our phones to hand. We have become purveyors of information, but without depth. We know very little about a lot. We became superficial. It was the eighteenth-century evangelist George Whitfield who said that God would not pour out his spirit on a superficial generation. We can split atoms, look into space, have conversations with people all over the world. We have so much accessibility to so much information. We thought that in the information world he who controls the information controls the world.

Information. Logically presented, systematically stated, with exceptional communication skills is the key to communicating Jesus. Paul knew it. In Athens he climbed on to a raised area and talked to them of the unknown God. He reasoned with them. He presented. And a few people came. We've trusted that approach for over a century. It's what courses like Alpha are based on. The approach goes, "If I can present and prove this then I can change this life." Not a criticism. It worked and it continues to work. But Paul walks into Corinth and knows that he had better change tack immediately. Same gospel, different approach. This is a hybrid community and this approach – logical, systematic, sequential presentation of truth – will not work here. And will shortly stop working in the twenty-first century.

Let me illustrate it to you. I give my most brilliant talk on who is Jesus. And you all nod and you get it. And I talk to you about why

Jesus died. And the presentation alone will cause you to say, "I get it. I understand it. I will commit to it." There will undoubtedly be many who became followers of Jesus as a result of a great Alpha talk. But the response in Corinth would have been very different, and has become the response today. We explain who Jesus is. And people get it. I explain why He died and they get that too. Therefore, why are they not on their knees giving their lives to Jesus? In an information age we just gave them more information and so they added it to what they already knew, but there was no transformation. It never moved beyond their heads. In Corinth, Paul is not trying to convince anyone. He does something so wonderfully brilliant. If I were there I promise you I would have applauded.

He shouts loudly: "This doesn't make sense, you cannot get it."

"Of course I can," comes the response. "This is the information age. I can get anything."

"Not this you can't. This particular miracle is complete foolishness."

Complete foolishness! You wouldn't make a religion like this. Buddha died at eighty, surrounded by a host of followers, Muhammad died at sixty-two, leader of a united Arabia, in the arms of his favourite wife. Jesus dies aged thirty-three with the might of the world, religious and political, hurling itself against a solitary figure. And in dying moments proclaims, "It is finished." C. S. Lewis, in *Mere Christianity*, nailed it for us when he said,

> The central Christian belief is that Christ's death has somehow put us right with God and given us a fresh start. Theories as to how it did this are another matter. A good many different theories have been held as to how it works; what all Christians are agreed on is that it does work... A man can eat his dinner without understanding exactly how food nourishes him. A man can accept what Christ has done without knowing how it works: indeed, he certainly would not know how it works until he has accepted it.[4]

Stop chasing heads. The world moved. It's time to become a heart hunter. Stop sucking the life out of the cross by trying to explain it.

---

4   *Mere Christianity*, New York: Macmillan Publishing Company Ltd, 1943, p. 64.

We're Called to Preach Awe, Wonder and Mystery. The Age of Information is Passing!

And the really cool part is that that is exactly what the school curriculum says are the hallmarks of a good school assembly. Wonder and awe. No, I do not know all the answers. I have spent six years in theological colleges and the best I can do is explain very articulately how much I don't know! But I do know that I am a passionate follower of Jesus and I know that He loves me unconditionally.

I was in Slough not so long ago, speaking in a homeless unit – lots of self-contained flats. It was Christmas and I'd been asked to come and explain what Christianity was all about. It was certainly a hostile crowd. The priest from the Sikh temple and the Muslim imam were also there, along with a man talking about Buddhism. The three other gentlemen went first and gave brilliant expositions of their belief systems. I told a story. A story of a little girl giving her dad a box of kisses for Christmas. I told them that God gave them a box of love as well. A gift named Jesus. No long explanations. But I know I won the day!

You and I are called to preach awe, wonder and mystery. The age of information is passing. We have to learn to experiment. We must learn not to be afraid of failure as we communicate into our deeply spiritual world.

Jesus cannot be explained. He cannot be neatly packaged. He cannot be summarized in a page on Wikipedia. But He does love you and He does love your community. And He can be encountered. He's not hiding. It's a mystery, everybody. Embrace it.

Vincent Donovan was a missionary to the Masai. He wrote *Christianity Rediscovered*. In his introduction to the second edition he wrote this advice regarding evangelism into our brave new world:

Do not try and call them back to where they were and do not try and call them to where you are as beautiful as that place might seem to you. You must have the courage to go with them to that place where neither you nor they have ever been before.[5]

Children's and Family Ministry Wasn't Like This When I Was Young

When considering ministry to children and families the average person could be forgiven for assuming that there are no positives. The media chooses to take a negative view of the influences on the child, the hostile world in which they live and the ineffective church that is haemorrhaging children at an alarming rate. Someone once commented, "The children now have bad manners and contempt for authority... Children are now tyrants." This is a quote from Plato. It's nearly 2,500 years old! It's used here to suggest that from the dawn of time children and childhood are often presented in a negative light, particularly by academics and even more particularly by the media. But it may not be quite what it seems. Lord Winston comments, "It's all very well to say that childhood depression is on the increase, but there are no data to support that."[6] Most read that sentence and are surprised. We have been hotwired to believe the negative. That's why we need our minds renewed. The reality is that bad news captures the public's attention. Good news rarely does. Let me prove it to you. When the Good Childhood Inquiry undertaken by The Children's Society launched in 2006 it captured huge media attention and predicted that we would at last recognize how terrible it is to be a child in the twenty-first-century. When the Inquiry presented its findings in 2014 and declared that boys and girls face a few difficult challenges but generally live safe and satisfying lives and that 87 per cent described themselves as happy, there was no front-page headline. No trumpeted announcement.

But what we can say with some authority is twenty-first century life is complicated! In 2010 only half of new mothers were married. Today, a quarter of children grow up with single parents. But what we mustn't do is draw a negative inference from this. Life is messy. Yes,

---

5   Donovan, V., *Christianity Rediscovered*, London: SCM Press, 1982.
6   Open letter to *The Guardian*, 18 September 2006.

children often live between two different homes because their parents have split up. But don't fall into the media trap. Don't think it's a problem when it's freely embraced. Today's generation of children will refuse the victim status that their parents and grandparents wore so freely; they are not wired to be victims. They are resilient. Children always have been, but more so with this generation who have become accustomed to relationships being radically integrated. They do take it in their stride. Beware the automatic assessment that they are broken and need ministry. If you look closely enough you'll discover they are full of joy.

I also hear a few comments with regard to how we interact with this generation: "We didn't used to do it like this." I've heard that a lot. The principle is the same for children's work as it is for every form of Christian ministry. We spent the last chapter revisiting the principle. **The message is timeless and unchanging, the style of presentation is linked to time and changes according to the culture**. Thomas Cranmer, 500 years ago, wrote:

> It is not necessary that customs and forms of worship be exactly the same everywhere. Throughout history they have differed. They may be altered according to nations, times and habits of people provided that nothing is commanded contrary to God's Word.[7]

We must work at being relevant and learn to start from where our audience is and not from where we are. The church has spent much time criticizing various children's work without realizing why millions of children are reading their books. Whether we like it or not, this is where the target audience is. It was sociologist Douglas Rushkoff who rightly pointed out that without moving an inch we have nonetheless travelled further than any other generation in history. This is not the generation of Enid Blyton's "Famous Five"; this is the generation of "Harry Potter" – the book series that Christians worked hardest to ban in the first decade of the twenty-first century (yes, there really is a list). I have defended the Harry Potter series diligently – not on the basis that there aren't some very concerning elements – but on the basis that we must start where this generation of children are at

---

7   Article 34 of Cranmer's 39 Articles of Religion.

and work from there. Throwing verbal stones at Harry Potter only alienates the very children we want to reach. At the same time the Harry Potter series gave such clear inroads for a presentation of the gospel I was almost grateful to Ms Rowling for writing it; we discover in *Goblet of Fire* the reason that Harry could not be hurt by Voldermot (I'm protected by an omnipotent God so I can get away with saying that name) when he was a baby. The reason being that somebody (in this case his mother) who loved him unconditionally was prepared to lay down her life for him! J. K. Rowling gives us a wonderful platform to present the gospel – I suspect unintentionally.

Every generation has different characteristics – some are good and some are bad – but on the whole they are what they are. And sometimes we must avoid value judgments until we dig beneath the surface. And it would have been the easiest thing in the world to simply list them here. But I don't know if that would help, so I've earthed each statement by attaching to it our response.

Superficial

Perhaps we can better designate this as the child's ability to become all things to all people. In the children's club they can answer the questions, sing the songs, and behave like an angel. In the classroom they can smile warmly, respond wholeheartedly, they work quietly. With their mates they can resort to a whole new vocabulary involving words that you didn't think they knew. They can be wild, have no respect for property, they can be basically sinful. And sometimes if we could see these children in these various settings outside the children's club we would be horrified at the apparent deception taking place.

Our response

I genuinely wish there was a shortcut here. But there isn't. What we mustn't do is question the fact that they have made a genuine decision to be a Christian simply because we see them behaving in a less than saintly manner elsewhere. Salvation may be instantaneous; sanctification is certainly not. Without feeling discouraged we simply keep doing what we do. We teach the truth because we know that ultimately it will overwhelm the lies. We keep on training the children in the way that they should go.

This generation is surprisingly sophisticated

The literature being written for this generation of children is complex – from Rowling to Womack. Today's children are clearly able to assimilate complex ideas, subtle plots and storylines that would not be out of place in a book for adults. Our approach to this generation must reflect this. What used to be the staple diet of eleven to fifteens is now what is being consumed by our eight to elevens.

Our response

The whole thing is moving forward at an alarming pace, and to keep relevant we have to immerse ourselves in the culture. That isn't as hard as it sounds. It simply means that we have to spend time with children, listen to the way they speak, look at the games they play, watch the programmes they watch, buy the music they are buying. My study has shelves and shelves of theology books, but it also has shelves and shelves of children's books – my latest addition is Frann Preston-Gannon's *Dave's Cave* (you'll love it!). We must continually update the work we do with children or very soon discover that we are no longer relevant and have drifted back into babysitting. But there is a warning. Don't try and be so relevant you forget that the gospel is always relevant. The way we present must change, what we present mustn't. It's quite a tightrope to walk.

This is a very discerning generation

If there has been a "disagreement" between two members of your team just before you open the doors to your children's club, the children will know. They don't need to be told, they don't need to have overheard, they will not be able to explain how they know, but they know. What's more it will affect them. The manipulative members of the group will work hard at keeping the disagreement alive and will pour as much salt on the wound as possible. The sensitive children will feel upset and become tearful. The rowdy children will become even rowdier. You are not in for a good evening.

Our response

The atmosphere the children walk into must be calm and peaceful. Some of these children are attending to escape the civil war they face in their homes on a regular basis; there is no place for war within the children's club. We must be a godly example as well as teach godly principles. What we are and what we say must never be contradictory.

This generation has no respect for authority

As in most of these areas, if we can take our model from Jesus then we can't go far wrong. Jesus could have presented the Sermon on the Mount like this: He could have asked one of His disciples to go on first and warm the crowd up and then the disciple could introduce Jesus: "Ladies and gentlemen, for one night only, for your entertainment, the King of Kings, the Prince of Peace, the Son of God, yes… here's Jesus." And then some angels would appear and blow trumpets; Jesus would descend on a cloud wearing His best white outfit and present the Sermon on the Mount. He could have. But He didn't. He stood as He was, He didn't make any claims. He simply stood and talked. He didn't hide behind His authority and the ordinary people flocked to hear Him.

Our response

To paraphrase the musician Sting, we should always be ourselves, whatever others might be saying. We never need to hide behind titles. One day the King of the Universe decided to adopt us as His son/daughter; He chose us, He reconciled us, He appointed us. We are His. We don't need to continually restate it, we just are it. When we walk into spiritual darkness the light within us dispels it, even before we begin to speak. This is who we are, we don't need to struggle or strive for prominence or position. How much higher could we get? So when we enter a school or a children's club or a conference we stand tall – Psalm 3:3 tells me that God is the glory and the lifter of my head. So we can stand tall and confident in who we are with no need for titles.

A headmaster in Doncaster once introduced me to his school with the words, "Boys and girls the Revd Dr Mark Griffiths has come to talk to you today and to tell what Christians believe." This was a headmaster who wasn't sure he wanted me in his school. He felt his chair of governors had forced me upon him and he was deliberately building a wall between the children and me. He understood exactly what he was doing. He understood what building me up as an authority figure would do. I walked to the front, smiled, and simply said, "Hi, my name's Mark. You can call me Mark because we are going to be friends and I've come to tell you what anyone with a brain would believe." And I turned and looked at the headmaster. It was a chilly few seconds, but he broke first and laughed out loud. The wall was broken. Communication was possible.

Total media exposure

Children today are exposed to all the great issues of life from a very early age: war, crime, sex, violence – they sit and digest it all on TV, or on YouTube, or whatever new media mechanism is created between me finishing typing and this book being published! They are bombarded with information at an alarming rate. Technology has become completely embedded in the everyday. A friend of ours phoned his wife recently using FaceTime™. The call was answered with the words, "Hello Daddy. Mummy is in the toilet." The little girl answering the iPhone™ is called Cesca; she will soon celebrate her second birthday.

Easy access. And of course the adage is true – if you are having trouble with your computer, ask a seven-year-old! The World Wide Web is the most natural way for them to gather information. The problem is this: knowledge does not equal wisdom. Children have a huge amount of information but don't know what to do with it or, more seriously, don't have the understanding to use that knowledge properly. In the Bible knowledge equals responsibility and responsibility denied brings guilt. Add to this the fact that children are now maturing earlier and we have an insight into the potential nightmare. Children becoming pregnant before they reach their teenage years; they know about the mechanics, they have knowledge, but no understanding of the consequences. Total media exposure is a time bomb waiting to explode. So far I suspect we have only seen a few hand grenades going off.

Our response

You will see in the section "The Programme" under "The Beginner's Guide..." (p. 21) that I advocate incorporating into the weekly children's programme a fun item called "Buy it or Bin it". It is a time when the children are allowed to listen to music that they would normally listen to, or watch a DVD clip of their favourite programmes or movies and then a panellist is asked whether they would buy the music/movie or whether they would bin it. They are then asked for a reason. They are not allowed to get away with "Because I don't like it." They must quantify their response a little better than that. "Buy it or Bin it" and items like it are more than fun items, they stimulate the children to develop something called "critical thought" – the ability not to allow tonnes of information to pour in, but to sift it, to analyse it, to evaluate it. With our own children we mustn't just switch channels when a bad programme comes on; we need to allow our children to understand why it isn't good for them to watch. When we watch adverts with our children, don't simply allow them to wash over you, talk about why the advert is good or bad.

All these things aid in the development of critical thought. Children are naturally sponge-like and will absorb anything. Guide them into a place of conscious choice with understanding. We are not just in the business of teaching; we are in the business of teaching them how to respond.

No cohesive metanarrative

I recently spoke at a Christian conference and stayed a few nights at a hotel. I arrived back late one night and I was more than a little surprised to see gentlemen rushing around in dinner suits followed closely by ladies in low-cut black dresses. I was a little concerned and was beginning to think I had entered the twilight zone. The truth turned out to be equally bizarre: the hotel I was staying at was staging a James Bond theme night! This was a cohesive metanarrative. A group of people from a diversity of backgrounds with something in common. By "metanarrative" we simply mean the common thread that connects people and forms them into communities rather than simply collections of individuals. I grew up in a Welsh valley where everyone knew everyone else. Not only did they know you, they knew your father and grandfather. At some point the whole valley had a common thread – the coal pit. Most of my friend's grandfathers had worked at it or in trades related to it. The valley still maintained its metanarratives. Small villages still to some extent hold on to their metanarrative and hence it is difficult for people to move into the community. However, this is becoming more and more rare and it takes very special events to give people a cohesive metanarrative.

In recent history, the death of Diana, Princess of Wales was one such occasion. Millions of people nationally and internationally were fused into communities with a common metanarrative; in this case their feelings of grief and loss. Unfortunately, the experience was short-lived and people quickly drifted back to being collections of individuals again. A similar occurrence took place in the aftermath of 9/11. It is a fact that more and more people are leaving villages all over the world and being drawn to large cities – huge people centres. The interesting thing is that across the world people are now living closer together than at any other point in history, yet they feel more isolated and more alone than at any other point of history.

Our response

The church has a major role to play in this whole area. For generations, the parish church existed as more than a place of worship; it existed as the place where the community came together. In my previous church I removed all the pews and refloored the inner area to make it possible to run large-scale youth, children and family events there. But I made it clear all along that we were not modernizing, we were removing the Victorian elements installed in the medieval building to make it once again the community hub it was built to be. The place where relationships were formed. The place where children experienced what it is to have a wider family – a wider family that provided support and care for the actual family. Through our wider activities, our community events, our all-age worship, we can reintroduce that common metanarrative. A community loving God and loving one another. Sound idealistic? Then let's work towards the ideal.

An erosion of moral absolutes

Society seems to do some strange things. In the last decade Holland legalized many hard drugs and then boasted to the rest of Europe that it had halved the number of convictions for drug offences. The amazing thing is that very few people saw the ridiculousness of the statement. The drug use hadn't changed, all that had changed was it was now legally allowed. We could take the label off the bottle of poison and relabel it as orange juice, it wouldn't change the fact that you would die if you drank it. What one generation tolerates the next generation accepts. We alive in an age where the maxim becomes "do what you want as long as you don't hurt anyone". If we say something is evil or wrong then society says we are evil!

But I have a caution here. I also don't believe in moral absolutes and I don't think Jesus did either. There are spiritual absolutes, but not moral ones. If there were then the woman caught in the act of adultery would have been stoned to death. She had broken the law. But Jesus constantly worked in the grey areas – I know that will be a shock to many but check it out. It was the Pharisees who dealt with moral absolutes.

Our response

WWJD. Not just a wristband, an actual way of behaving. What would Jesus do when faced with the current situation, this complex moral dilemma? What would Jesus do? My previous church had a lesbian couple. How do we respond? They had a daughter. It also had several couples living together who weren't married. Is that worse or better? Are there levels of sin? All theology is practical theology. It must work in the real world. No point in having a moral code that doesn't work. So we ask ourselves again and again, what would Jesus do? We will need to constantly revisit our theology in the coming decades, so hold it lightly and keep asking the key question.

But allow me to leave this chapter with a piece of homework for you. Please think of a child. A specific child. One you know. And then answer some questions:

SOCIOLOGY 101

Stage 1

Picture a child. They need to be an actual child between the ages of four and fourteen.

How old are
they?

What is their
name?

Who do they
live with?

What do they
do in their free
time?

What do they
watch on TV?

What is their
favourite
food/drink?

What Bible story
would you tell
them? Why?

What is their
attitude to a)
parents b) friends?

What is their
attitude to God?

Where do they
spend their
time?

What is their
attitude to the
opposite sex?

What influences
them?

What do they
talk about ?

Stage 2

- Has anything surprised you?
- What are you certain of, and what were you less certain of? How can you confirm your data?

Stage 3:

- How are these children developing cognitively? Maybe refer to the theology lectures?
- How are they developing socially? Toward parents, adults, friends...
- How are they developing physically?
- How are they developing spiritually?
- What Bible stories will you use when you talk to them? Why? How can you provide them?
- How are they becoming aware of their world?

Congratulations. You're a sociologist. And your findings are as valuable as any of the findings that you will discover in tomorrow's papers.

Section 1
Children's Ministry in Four Dimensions

Author Philip Cliff concluded his PhD on the Sunday school movement with the words, "Sunday School teachers cannot do for parents what they must do for themselves. The classroom is no substitute for the family."

It's a popular view and one with which most would certainly agree. But his statement does need further analysis. If we dig a little deeper into this word "family" we will quickly discover that there are at least two Hebrew words that are translated into the English word "family". And a closer inspection quickly reveals that there are interesting nuances that give us some insight. The following chapters will look at these nuances.

This section therefore looks at Children's Ministry in four dimensions. Three dimensions look at the context of our work with children and families:

- Home – the immediate family
- Home – the wider family or church community
- The world – communicating the Jesus story to boys and girls who wouldn't hear about it in any other way.

And then an introduction to the fourth dimension. The one that holds the rest together, the one on whom the other dimensions stand or fall:

- The parent or children and family worker – basically: YOU!

The First Dimension—*Bah'ith* תַּיִב

The first word translated "family" is the word *bah'ith* תַּיִב. *Bah'ith* communicates the concept of what we would now call the immediate family – parents and children together under one roof. We encounter this word in the instructions for the Passover meal (Exodus 12:21–28). On the very first Passover, a lamb was sacrificed and the blood of that lamb placed on the doorpost of individual homes. Inside those homes, the lamb was then made into a family meal that the Hebrew family celebrated gathered together around the table. This first Passover was the night of liberation, the night of freedom, and God instructed them to continue to celebrate this meal every year to remember what God had done. It's instituted to remind the Hebrews (in the context of *bah'ith*) that they don't serve a passive God, but an active God. The God who does things.

So every year for over 3,000 years, Jews have sat down together and celebrated Passover. It is a liturgical ceremony because at the appointed time during the meal the youngest child stands and asks, "What makes this night special?", thus allowing the father or mother to make his or her liturgical response by explaining the story of the Passover and of the exodus. Emphasizing that they serve an active God, not just a God who does things, but a God who is doing things, a God endowed with potentiality – God was active in the past, is active now and will be active in the future.

This communication of the God who is active is fundamental to everything we do. "The God who does stuff" is how I usually put it. Theologically we don't believe in the God who creates the universe and then walks away from His creation allowing the whole thing to wind down over several millennia as the forces of entropy do their work. We don't believe that theologically, but sometimes we seem to communicate that in our practice. This is the God who creates and steps into His creation. The God who shows up. The God who can change things. We must communicate this to our children. When I was working as a children's pastor in Milton Keynes I ran an event called "Frantic" for primary school children. Over 200 children came every Saturday morning. Several days before one of these Saturdays I had been to preach at a large church that had just purchased a video projector. To give you some idea of when this was, the video projector had three coloured lights at the front! You could probably see one today in the British Museum (I've been around for a while!).

At this point I was in my early twenties and still slightly naive. I came back to "Frantic" and asked the children if we should pray and ask God for one as well – after all, this is the God who does things! We prayed. Two hundred children and I prayed.

The following morning I preached in the Sunday services. At the end of the service someone came up to me and told me that God had asked them to give me something. He handed me a cheque for £2,000 with the words, "You know what it's for." I did! I purchased the projector and the following Saturday morning I put it on. Slowly (very slowly) the picture emerged on the projector screen. The children went silent. They stared. I explained, "Last week we prayed and God sent the money, so we could purchase one of these." They started to exchange various versions of the word "Wow!" and then one little seven-year-old boy on the front row put his hand up and said, "Mark, Mark, what else can God do?"

And that's the point. The God who does things. Endowed with potentiality. What else can He do?

That's an example in the context of a children's club but the same principle is supposed to be at the heart of the home. Our children are supposed to hear the stories of how God provides for us. I tell them of the time in theological college when I had no grant and no income how God provided the final payment for my fees on the day of graduation. This was in the days when things were a little tougher and if you hadn't paid the fees you weren't going to graduate. And on graduation day, at lunchtime, the principal came to find me to tell me the final payment had just been handed to him. I still have no idea where it came from. But my children hear this story because I want them to know the God who does stuff. My wife and I often talk about the way God has provided for us. At the time of writing I have just handed in my resignation as senior minister of the largest Anglican church in Berkshire. It's a job that comes with accommodation in a very nice vicarage. There is a regular monthly salary. And now we've laid it all down. We're not sure what is next. But it's going to be a great opportunity to once again show our children the God who does stuff.

The earlier followers of Jesus would continue this practice of communicating the active God, but the stories would be added to. Not only would the account of the Passover and exodus be recounted, but now also the Son of God, Jesus who became flesh, who walked on water, fed thousands, healed the sick, raised the dead, was crucified, and resurrected. The *bah'ith* context remains the same, the principle of the communication of an active God remains the same, but the stories change and added to those stories are personal accounts of how God helped that family.

Today across the planet followers of Jesus gather in the context of *bah'ith* and exchange stories – stories of the Passover and exodus, stories of incarnation and resurrection, and new stories to the God who heals, empowers His church, and does miracles today.

All about the family

This focus on the home is of huge importance, yet it is not an area we give enough attention to. The work of child evangelism and children's groups are areas that I am so excited about and which we will cover in the next chapters. They are incredibly positive but in terms of ministry within the home there were some negatives. They could be summarized as follows:

- the place of teaching moved from the home to a building
- the time for teaching moved from "day" to "day" to Sunday
- the teacher was no longer the parent but the professional children's worker.

The communication about Jesus in the home seems to have become a lost art. And also something that is seen as a little scary. Let me see if I can take the intensity away if nothing else. I have three children. Nia is twenty; the one who has just returned from Australia working as an intern at Edge Church, Adelaide. To keep this in perspective for you, when I told her at dinner that I was writing this chapter, she looked around the table at her brothers and said, "Have you really thought this through?"

Her brother Owen is eighteen. When he was fourteen he outworked his teenage rebellion by leaving the parish church I was leading and insisted on walking the two miles every Sunday to one of our church plants. He now gets to preach and lead there. He has concluded that he doesn't mind when I come to preach because at least it means he doesn't have to walk.

Elliot is fifteen and the primary reason I didn't write the good parenting guide! He recently received a school report that alongside nearly every subject had the words, "Elliot must do better." At the end of the report was a section for Elliot to complete to explain what he would do differently the following term. It was all laid out for him. His head of year wanted him to write the words "I will do better", his mother and I wanted him to write the words "I will do better". We left him to think about what he should write. We gave him plenty of clues, but left him with the final decision as to what to write. When I returned an hour later to see his response I read these words, "I will join more after-school clubs!"

My children are all different. Very individual. Different motivators, different temperaments, but all great fun. But this paragraph is here for one reason only, to say to you that I am trying to work this out too. And so this chapter will not be a spiritual rampage on why you must have family prayers for two hours every day. Because I can't teach what I can't do. It'll be a gentle walk through this important area of communicating faith in the home, in the context of *bah'ith*.

Edward Gibbon, in his book *The History of the Decline and Fall of the Roman Empire*, comments that part of the reason for the destruction of Rome was that it no longer had strong families and therefore the empire fell from within. John Chrysostom, the fourth-century bishop writes:

> To each of you fathers and mothers I say, just as we see artists fashioning their paintings and statues with great precision, so we must care for these wondrous statues of ours. Painters when they have set the canvas on the easel paint on it day by day to accomplish their purpose. Sculptors, too, working in marble,

proceed in a similar manner; they remove what is superfluous and add what is lacking. Even so you must proceed. Like the creators of statues do you give all your leisure to fashioning these wondrous statues for God.

Proverbs 22:6 speaks of training up a child in the way they should go, and when they are old they will not depart from it. What is interesting there is the "the way *they* should go". Rather than dictating that they need to get a proper job – whatever that may mean – we should help them seek and discern what God has created them to be and do. John Chrysostom again speaks of parents' "vainglory" in trying to push their children into certain well-paying, high-visibility roles. Those fourth-century pushy parents, hey!

My contention in this area really is that if you understand "WHY" then you'll work out "HOW?" I became a Christian when I was fifteen. My wife grew up in a nominally Christian Welsh Baptist home; we were first generation followers of Jesus. We had no real blueprint. We were working out how to be a family as we went. I had some advantages – I had been employed as a children's pastor for six years by then, so I knew that reading them stories from Leviticus might not be a good idea. And Bob Hartman had managed to publish his *Storyteller Bible* so reading material was freely available. But we really did have to work it out. When I grew up if I was unwell my parents phoned the doctor, nobody prayed for me. At bedtime I found a book to read. At mealtime, my sister and I just ate, nobody said grace. We often ate on trays in front of the television. Not a lot of conversation except on Sundays.

So we had to introduce things into our family. Grace at meals. Bedtime stories from the Bible or one of a million Christian books that I love. When our children were ill we would take them to the doctor, but we would pray first. When they had bad dreams we would pray and inform them with a theology learned from Veggie Tales that "God is bigger than the bogeyman." And when Nia went to Australia we gathered around her as a family in the middle of Heathrow airport and we prayed.

But we have an increasing number of first generation Christians. It's a positive. It means we are reaching the lost. But we also want to have lots and lots of second and third and fourth generation followers, so we need to pass on faith. And allow me to be candid. This really isn't about building in some sort of insurance policy that says my kids must be Christians or they'll not go to heaven when they die. This is about bringing your children up in the presence of Jesus so that they become everything God created them to be right now. It's about the Holy Spirit shaping and forming and sculpting them so they live well – knowing how to deal with hurt and pain and disappointment, responding with compassion and love and grace. Generous, forgiving and gracious – right now. Living life with the quality of eternity – right now. It is about instilling in them an understanding that they are loved, valued and accepted... even if they walk away and become one of the prodigals.

And this is really not about making perfect human beings. If I do this right they'll be in the Olympics aged thirteen and Oxbridge shortly after. It isn't about overprotecting and keeping them away from the harsh realities of this cruel world. They are naturally resilient. If you could listen to the newborn baby it would be saying the words, "Bring it on!" Doctors will tell you that poorly babies are the best fighters. They want to do life.

Brené Brown, in her incredible book *Daring Greatly* (you must read it), says this:

> When it comes to parenting, the practice of framing mothers and fathers as good or bad is both rampant and corrosive—it turns parenting into a shame minefield. The real questions for parents should be: "Are you engaged? Are you paying attention?" If so, plan to make lots of mistakes and bad decisions. Imperfect parenting moments turn into gifts as our children watch us try to figure out what went wrong and how we can do better next time. The mandate is not to be perfect and raise happy children. Perfection doesn't exist, and I've found that what makes children happy doesn't always prepare them to be courageous, engaged adults.[8]

Until recently I sat as a Family Court magistrate. On various occasions, I would get slightly concerned when a social worker would be asked about the standard of care in a particular family and they would respond, "It's good enough." Eventually I challenged it only to be told in no uncertain terms by a very experienced social worker that, "Good

---

8   Brown, Brené, *Daring Greatly*, London: Penguin, 2015, p. 15.

enough is really rather good." But it's not perfect. Perfection may just be our enemy. To be perfect parents is not the goal. Good enough is really rather good.

But maybe we can uncover a few more keys. Here's the hardest: absolute acceptance. Chrysostom gives us a bit more insight from the fourth century when he speaks of the love from parent to child being the same as God's love to us. *Agape* love. Unconditional love. Green hair, pierced nose and/or belly button, inappropriate boyfriend, needing improvement in every possible school subject... absolute acceptance. We have to communicate that we accept their imperfections. And they are worth loving. It's the essence of *bah'ith*. Acceptance is a massive word. And the tension of controlling your facial muscles when they walk into the room in a clothing range that in all honesty you are struggling with. Don't let your face give you away. Absolute acceptance, not "Wish you were taller, smaller, thinner, smarter, tidier, more Christian, attended church more..."

As I said, I'm from a Welsh valley. I left in the late 1980s. As 2016 wasn't the easiest year for us, I returned often to that place of absolute acceptance. There in that little valley I am accepted, not because of what I've done. They've only ever heard me preach at the occasional funeral and family baptism; they've never read my books. I have a PhD, eight published books, spoken all over the world, led one of the largest churches. They don't care. Really! I'm accepted because of who I am. I was born there. My family are there – my *bah'ith*. Our children need to feel absolute acceptance because they are family. Because of who they are. Our *bah'ith*. And of course, there is a delightful trap built into this: it's only possible to accept your children fully if you have learned to accept yourself. Otherwise you'll constantly see your faults in them. Ultimately the key lies in being the sort of person you want your children to become. What do you model when it all goes wrong? What do you model when it all goes right?

A few more keys. Are you engaged? Are you involved? Are you there? Not physically there – we can all manage that sometimes – but are you wholly there: body, mind and spirit? Are you truly engaged in the job of being the parent God called you to be? Engagement means investing time and energy. It means sitting down with our children and understanding their worlds, their interests, and their stories.

I read an interesting story recently about a man who was determined to win the affection of a lady who refused to even talk to him. He decided that his only option was to write to her, and to keep writing to her. So he began writing her love letters. He wrote a love letter every day. Six, seven times a week she got a letter from him. When she still didn't acknowledge him he started writing three letters a day. This went on for three years. He wrote her thousands of letters. And at the end of the three years there was a wedding. The lady married the postman! Letters, gifts, emails, all good, but none of them stand up to being there. Not always getting it right, rarely perfect, but present.

This is possibly the hardest thing to do at this point in history. We have forgotten how to be fully present. When I was learning to snowboard my instructor gave me one simple piece of advice, "You'd be great at this if your mind was actually here rather than thinking about a dozen other things. Focus on this, just this." It worked. And my snowboarding is still so poor that it has become one of my favourite things to do. Why? Because I can't focus on a dozen other things and stay upright. I have to be fully present. It's a skill to learn.

Rob Bell remains one of my heroes. In his recent book *How to Be Here*, he said this, "When you are constantly judging what you're doing you aren't here. You aren't present. You are standing outside of your life, looking in, observing."[9]

There is a fascinating commentary on the story of Moses and the burning bush. The rabbis say that the bush didn't suddenly start burning when Moses came to it; it had been burning the whole time. Moses was simply moving slowly enough and paying attention enough to actually notice it.

I'm taking for granted that we are modelling prayer and reading our Bibles. But in passing I have discovered the key to prayer! It's quite simple. Set aside a time of day to meet with God and ALWAYS keep the appointment. There will be days when the heavens seem as brass, there will be days when you feel that God has forsaken you, there will be days of joy and peace in His presence, but all you must do is be there. Keep the appointment. Everything else can flow from there. If you don't keep the appointment, that's when the cracks appear. Just be there at the time you told God you would be.

---

9   *How to Be Here*, London: HarperOne, 2016, p. 102.

And now with full acknowledgment that this chapter could take up the entire book, here are my four summary principles:

- good enough is really rather good – don't chase perfection
- absolute acceptance is *the* key
- be the sort of person you want your children to become
- be fully present.

And none of this in any way opens the door to guilt. If you've not been good at this, then start now. But neither does it give a guarantee. But I wholeheartedly agree with our bishop Chrysostom, that when we are fully engaged in parenting, regardless of how imperfect, vulnerable and messy it is, we are creating something sacred. And if your *bah'ith* already has parts that are not following Jesus – who don't turn up in church as much as you would like; who despite your best efforts have drifted away – there is no guilt. If they have moved into the realms of the prodigals, we need to continue to outwork our four principles above, and to pray and wait patiently and believe for the prodigals to return.

Not perfect parents. Just real ones. And to help us understand what *real* is here's an extract from Margery Williams' amazing book *The Velveteen Rabbit*:

"Real isn't how you are made," said the Skin Horse. "It's a thing that happens to you. When a child loves you for a long, long time, not just to play with, but really loves you, then you become Real."

"Does it hurt?" asked the Rabbit.

"Sometimes," said the Skin Horse, for he was always truthful. "When you are Real, you don't mind being hurt."

"Does it happen all at once, like being wound up," he asked, "or bit by bit?"

"It doesn't happen all at once," said the Skin Horse. "You become. It takes a long time. That's why it doesn't often happen to people who break easily, or have sharp edges, or who have to be carefully kept. Generally, by the time you are Real, most of your hair has been loved off, and your eyes drop out, and you get loose in the joints and very shabby. But these things don't matter at all, because once you are Real, you can't be ugly, except to people who don't understand."[10]

---

10 Williams, Margery, *Velveteen Rabbit*, New York: George H. Doran Company, 1922.

The Second Dimension– Mish-paw-khaw הָחְפִּשְׁמ

Bah'ith is not the word most commonly translated "family" in the Old Testament – that honour goes to the word *mish-paw-khaw* (הָחְפִּשְׁמ). This word carries within it the sense of clan or community; it is in effect a bond of kinship uniting people to a common cause. Deuteronomy 6:5–7 and Deuteronomy 11:18–19, when instructions are given for the passing on of the belief system from one generation to the next, are written in the context of *mish-paw-khaw*.

That which constitutes a *family* in the Old Testament is the bond of kinship that unites its members; *mish-paw-khaw* includes all those to whom that kinship extends. So when a Hebrew boy reached the age of marriage he would travel to the home of his wife-to-be and propose (weddings were usually arranged by the parents, so his proposal was a sure thing!). Once she had formally accepted and hung the lit lantern in her window to indicate that she was now engaged, the young Hebrew man would return to the family home and begin the construction of a new set of rooms added onto the family home, or a new house next to the family home. When the home was completed, the bride would then move to her new home (via a week of celebrations). Other sons within the same house would be doing a similar thing and in turn the son's sons would follow that same pattern. Over time what started out as a family would become an extended family, a further extended family and eventually would become a whole tribe (Hebrew archaeology supports this, with archaeological digs revealing a central older residence and newer residences emanating out from there). The word used to describe this group of people that could number thousands was *mish-paw-khaw*. And every member of this *mish-paw-khaw* recognized their responsibility to communicate the faith of the *mish-paw-khaw* to the children of that *mish-paw-khaw*.

This pattern was continued by the early followers of Jesus. When they gathered in Solomon's colonade (Acts 5:12) as this new Jesus *mish-paw-khaw*, there would have been children present and all the members of this new Jesus community recognized their responsibility to communicate the Jesus story into the lives of the children of this newly formed *mish-paw-khaw*.

And of course, while the *bah'ith* looks like our modern families, *mish-paw-khaw* looks like church: a gathering of people united together with a common cause. And in the same way that all the members of the original *mish-paw-khaw* recognized their responsibility to communicate the faith to the new generation, so should the members of our congregations. But it is slightly subtler than that. The Jewish understanding is that the whole community *do* communicate – whether they choose to or not. Not just the children's team! *All the members communicate.* Our attitudes, our passions, our commitments, the way we worship, the way we respond to others, all communicate to the children of *mish-paw-khaw*.

Everyone in *mish-paw-khaw* communicates to the children of *mish-paw-khaw* not just the children's team. So that cantankerous man who sits on the front row who is constantly complaining that we don't sing enough hymns communicates his frustration into the lives of the boys and girls of that *mish-paw-khaw*. At the same time that newly married couple who know that they maybe should be putting in more overtime at work because they could do with the extra money, but instead choose to miss out on extra income for the sake of the worship practice – when they stand in front of the church on Sunday morning they communicate their love and sacrifice into the boys and girls of the *mish-paw-khaw*. None of them are in the children's teams or in the youth teams, but that doesn't matter – everyone who is part of *mish-paw-khaw* communicates to the boys and girls of that *mish-paw-khaw*.

To belong to *mish-paw-khaw* is a privilege, but it is a privilege that comes with responsibility. When was the last time you heard someone preach that message, "To be part of this church community is a privilege, but it is a privilege that comes with responsibility." Freedom in Christ means we have liberty to say what we want. That really doesn't mean we should say what we want. We are responsible for our attitudes in front of that rising generation. But more than that. There are subtleties to this supernatural *mish-paw-khaw* system that slip past us. When we stand at the front of our churches every week and give heartfelt pleas for people to help with the children's groups because "if nobody helps we will not be able to run." That sends the most terrible message to the boys and girls of that *mish-paw-khah*. If you have heard begging messages proclaimed week after week in a desperate attempt to get people to come and look after you, what are you eventually going to conclude? Nobody wants to be with me. I am not wanted here. It would be better if I wasn't here. Can we really blame them when they are ten or eleven that they decide to stop attending church? Let me suggest some words. If you do have a gap in your Sunday morning rota go with:

Ladies and gentlemen, we have an opportunity for you to be involved in one of the most exciting ministries in the church this morning. You'll not only make a difference now, you'll change the future. We need a helper for the five to sevens!

In fairness I recruit for the coffee rota with a fair amount of passion too. But that's because I think more churches would see revival if they invested in some decent coffee!

The following chapters are *mish-pah-khaw* chapters: children and family ministry in the context of the gathered Christian community in a certain place. That thing you and I call the local church. The thing that pastor Bill Hybels describes as the hope of the world.

The Challenge of Intergenerational Worship

Many ministers – and for that matter – family workers approach the idea of intergenerational worship with great trepidation. It is true to say that done badly the intergenerational service can be a nightmare; done well it can be transformative. There are many publications that will provide insights into putting together an all-age worship service, but to make two main points:

- Inviting all the families that you have contact with to an all-age service is a good way of familiarizing them with the church and the people who attend. The first visit is often the hardest, and once people have been they may be more inclined to come back.
- The Sticky Faith[11] research was very clear: **those who experience more intergenerational worship tend to have higher faith maturity**.

It clearly isn't an optional extra. If you want to connect with families who don't normally attend Sunday congregations, and you want children who attend to have a mature faith, then intergenerational worship is the way to go. I think it true to say that there have now emerged different "types" of church-based intergenerational service/gathering; the first is the "all-age worship" service that takes place on Sunday mornings. It may happen every week as proponents of intergenerational worship champion, or once a month as is the pattern

---

11   Sticky Faith is a research initiative of the Fuller Youth Institute based at Fuller Theological Seminary in California. The research looked at the methods of passing on faith from one generation to the next. The research is ongoing, but the results so far have produced a range of resources that have been seen to be successful in the communication of faith. These resources are published under the title of "Sticky Faith".

in many Anglican churches (curiously, usually the first Sunday) as part of the overall Sunday morning diet, with children going out to their own age-specific groups on other Sundays. There is another category in this type – churches that do "occasional all-age services" for events such as Easter, Harvest and Christmas. Other than the already made point on the importance of intergenerational worship I'll not express a view on how often it should take place.

However, there has now emerged a second "type" of intergenerational gathering – exemplified by Messy Church. I think we have to use the Messy Church label because even those projects that don't use the name Messy Church often use the format. There is of course an overlap in that many churches run Messy Church as their Sunday morning worship service or as their monthly all-age service (in many ways "Explore Together", the new Scripture Union resource, has repackaged Messy Church to be used in the "main" worship service, but its focus on different learning styles is really helpful). More generally Messy Church takes place outside the conventional Sunday morning meeting slot, often monthly on Sunday afternoons, and certainly at inception its primary audience was not those who regularly attend the Sunday morning worship services (although many families attend both). And of course, as is the way with these things, Messy Church has evolved and, in many places, has become church in its own right rather than the assumed bridge into church.

The following paragraphs will look at both these types of church.

All-age service (as part of the Sunday morning worship service)

Firstly, an opt out. "Explore Together" by Scripture Union and countless other resources are completely given over to this area. There are simply a few pointers in the *mish-pah-khaw* section of this book. So here we go:

- This is not an adult service with a children's slot nor is it a children's service. It's all-age worship. We are singing the songs together, we are learning from the message together, we are responding to that message together, from the youngest to the oldest.
- Use a handout with quiz, colouring, etc., when people arrive. Use interaction throughout – children and adults together leading prayers.

- You don't have to wear silly trousers, a funny tie or a red nose! Be yourself. Children will see through you otherwise.
- Use prizes as an incentive – children and adults will approve.
- Use a story or parable for the talk/preach. This is Jesus' primary communication vehicle. He could communicate with the youngest and the oldest at the same time using this medium. Look at the story of the prodigal or the good Samaritan. They are interesting and accessible for all ages.
- Finish the entire service within forty-five minutes unless you have an activity time that involves people making things together.
- You will have all sorts of learning styles represented. Make sure you have something to look at, have something to do.
- Use film clips. But don't do death by PowerPoint. One or two PowerPoint words to direct people is fine. Forty-seven key points on the construction of the tabernacle is not.
- I hate to admit it, but you can wing it when it comes to conventional, liturgical services. People will know if you haven't prepared for an all-age service, though. You have to do the preparatory work or it will show.
- Create an all-age team and share out parts of the service between yourselves while also involving the congregation. Multiple people and personalities will keep it interesting.
- There are a lot of ingredients to choose from:
- games
- quizzes
- interactive prayers
- movie clips
- activities (make something individually or as teams – make a palm cross or a Christingle for example)
- discuss with neighbour/small group/shout answers to front
- tell stories using people as characters (use costumes)
- use object lessons, props, magic tricks.

And when you think it's gone wrong, it may be the finest moment! My favourite all-age talk ever took place at a Bible week at a very well-known holiday camp:

The story of Elijah on Mount Carmel was being told. It was incredible. Key church leaders were roped in to play various characters. National leaders were made to wear a pantomime cow outfit. The work had been done. Elijah was ready to call fire down from heaven. He instructed the sacrifice be covered in water first, but of course the person playing Elijah had covered the sacrifice in some flammable liquid. He had a lighter behind his back ready to call down fire as he threw the flame onto the flammable liquid. He had practised it so many times. There were several thousand people in the audience of all ages. And that was undoubtedly the thing that made him do it. The extra crowd made him a little overexcited. So he'd placed more flammable liquid than usual onto the sacrifice. Then came the moment. Elijah called fire from heaven, he threw the flame, the liquid caught fire, there was a huge whoosh as the flames took to the air, the audience gasped, it was truly amazing. And then the flames rose higher... and the curtains that surrounded the stage caught fire. So imagine the scene. Elijah is in the centre, the paddling pool that contained the flammable liquid is a huge fire, but framing the whole thing are flames right around the curtains which are on the left, on the right and up above. People rushed in from all directions with fire extinguishers to put out the flames. The audience stared in stunned silence. Then one after another got to their feet and applauded the best all-age talk they had ever heard. The children will never forget it, neither will the adults.

The effect was unforgettable and spectacular, but it was all reasonably simple to do. A well-known story, a few costumes and a couple of props. See what you can do? Although it may be best to avoid fire!

And one final comment: be realistic, not everyone can do it! It's just the way it is. Some of your most gifted preachers are hopeless at all-age. And it is not age dependent. I've seen plenty of "young" people be hopeless at all-age and plenty of "old" people nail it every time. Simply remember to work to people's strengths.

The Sunday morning children's programme

But let's not throw out the proverbial baby with the bathwater. I am a strong advocate of intergenerational worship, and I know many who would suggest that all our services should be intergenerational. I am not one of them. A balanced diet, in my opinion, involved intergenerational worship and single generation teaching groups.

At home there are times when we gather as a family to do things intergenerationally. Usually this involves food, but increasingly the cinema has been getting a lot more family visits. But there are also times when my children withdraw to their own rooms and my wife and I withdraw to a different room. This is called family. We do some things together, some things independently. Church family is undoubtedly the same. Some things community, some things as youth, or children, or young adults, etc.

So Sunday morning children's ministry has its place as part of a balanced church diet. But some definitions are needed; by Sunday morning children's programme we are talking about the activity that takes place on Sunday mornings when the adults are in their meeting. It is usually relatively short (unless you happen to be taking the group when an overenthusiastic preacher is on). The children who attend will be primarily from Christian families.

To state again, this section is here because of its importance to the overall picture. A survey of those who had recently joined a new church cited **the quality of the Sunday morning children's ministry as being the second most important thing they looked for when seeking to join a church** (number one was the quality of the preaching). Don't skip over that statistic; if your Sunday morning children's provision is not good, then people will consciously choose to go to a different church because of this. And don't get too hung up on that fact that the statement sounds consumeristic. When people first look to join a church, that's exactly what they are, consumers. Only the gospel will lead them to becoming producers.

The whole programme must work together. Children who start attending your outreach club, who make decisions for Jesus, who bring their families along on Sunday will now go to the Sunday morning children's programme. So is the Sunday morning children's programme about babysitting? Yes! Should our attitude when we come to teach this group be one of babysitting? Absolutely not!

Don't get hung up on this, you must see the balance. There must be an element of babysitting. We should be caring for children in a safe and secure environment while their parents listen to the preaching. Our room, our staffing, our environment, our safety procedure all reflect the best babysitting service in the world. However, our teaching and our communication must reflect a heartfelt desire to use every single opportunity given to us to win and disciple boys and girls for Jesus.

This chapter should not be read in isolation; many of the programme items outlined in the outreach club format will fit perfectly well here – the time issue obviously doesn't allow for the play element; the chapters on leaders and vision are particularly appropriate. But there are some issues which are unique to this area and it is to these that we will now turn our attention.

How do we split the ages?

This can be quite a challenge. You could have everything from nought to fourteen (children older than fourteen should be encouraged to stay in the service, or be working as junior leaders). The education system has already done the majority of the work for us, the split I suggest is:

0 – 3s	Crèche
3 – 4s	Pre-school group
5 –11s	Primary school group (Key Stage 1 & 2 in UK)
11–14s	Secondary school group

Probably the first task is to rename the groups to something a little more dynamic than "Pre-school group"! And at the same time a name for the whole programme may be useful. This will give the group an identity. But caution is needed – names that incorporate "school" send out the wrong message; names such as "junior church" are simply theologically unsound – the children's gathering represents church, there is no such thing as a junior version.

The previous chapters have already outlined my feelings on the need for a team of people working in each of the groups rather than one person sat on a seat, but let me re-emphasize that to sit one person on a seat with a specific age group is not only ineffective, it is also contrary to the child protection policies of most churches. The younger the age groups the more critical this becomes; in the pre-school group it may be necessary to take the children to the toilet, in the crèche it may become necessary to change nappies. Your workers must be police checked by the Disclosure and Barring Service (DBS) and no group should ever be staffed by only one person.

When do the children go to their children's programme slot?

Do the children go straight to their groups and not join with the adults at all? Do they go to their groups every week?

When my children's friends come to visit, my house seems to very naturally split into age groups. The children play in the playroom or in one of the bedrooms. I am very happy about this; I work with children much of the time, it is sometimes a delight to be left in a room by myself. However, much I love my moments of solitude (increasingly rare though they are) my children will never learn anything from me if I keep them in a separate room all the time. It is very important that the children see adults worshipping. It is vitally important that at least once a quarter children stay in for the whole service and that the service takes on an "all-age flavour".

What should the format of the morning children's programme be?

There is a limited period of time, but I still suggest using a condensed version of the "The Programme" outline listed in "The Beginner's Guide" section (p. 219). Start the sessions with prayer and children's praise songs. Because the songs cut across the age groups it is good to have the three and four-year-olds mixed in with the five to elevens for the singing. After ten to fifteen minutes of prayer and songs the three- and four-year-olds move off to their group. The eleven to fourteens go straight to their group – with all the hormones flying around this group it is probably best to send them to the youth specialists as soon as possible!

Use whatever incentive is appropriate to the size of the group, but a positive reinforcement method should be used.

What teaching materials do we use?

The prayer, praise, games, etc., format advocated in a later section should be used at the start of the programme, but the second section – the teaching programme – could be taken from countless publications. There are many options as you will see if you visit your local Christian bookshop. The material that suits your group is the best material to use. You may need to experiment. Options include:

- *Roots* – www.rootsontheweb.com
- *Light* – www.scriptureunion.org.uk/light/
- *Living Stones* – www.kevinmayhew.com/living-stones-complete-resource-a.html#.WRxMOOvyvIU
- *Children's Ministry* – www.handinhandconference.com/
- *Go Teach* - www.goteach.org.uk
- *Fusion*, *Impact* and *Detonate* by Mark Griffiths – online or from your local Christian bookshop

And finally: Keep the profile of children's ministry high on the church's agenda.

- If the children leave partway through the service, the presiding minister should pray for the children and the children's leaders as they leave for their groups.
- At least once a year the church's vision for young people and children should be presented to the whole church.
- The church council should allocate a reasonable budget to the children and family programme and a very healthy budget for training for this area.

Lost in Transition – Jo Foster

Over the last decade much has been done to raise the position of family, youth and children's work within the church. Many churches now employ both youth and family/children's pastors, more funds are being invested in this ministry and there has been a clear shift away from seeing children's work as merely childminding – to a ministry which invests in the spiritual life of children and young people. Despite the investment that churches are making, there is a clear age-related problem which neither the employment of a children's nor youth pastor has resolved – and that is that many children who are either brought up in the Sunday schools or attend weekly outreach events do not continue into the youth or adult church when they begin their transition from primary to secondary school.

Peter Brierley refers to this age group as the "tweenager" – young people aged between eight and thirteen. Tweenagers are in between childhood and adolescence – a good definition of this age group would be "those who buy merchandise to look, dress and act like teenagers". These are the group who have clearly outgrown children's ministry but are often too young for youth ministry.

The loss of this age group is not a recent problem – Peter Brierley carried out extensive research in 2002 (*Reaching and Keeping Tweenagers*) which was instigated from the 1998 "English Church Attendance Survey" which had highlighted that the number of under fifteens in the church had dropped by nearly half a million in the previous nine years. According to Brierley, "the church is haemorrhaging young people. We were losing 1000 under 15 years a week." Brierley's research led to startling results – the majority of kids who go to church had stopped between their tenth and eleventh birthday; not only that – 57 per cent of children who leave churches do so before their tenth birthday.

Nearly twenty years on, losing children in the move from primary to secondary is still a real issue. According to Christian Research the church in the UK will have lost an estimated 1.1 million children between 1990 and 2020. They also predict that in the year 2020, 183,700 children under fifteen will attend church compared to 375,300 in 2010.[12]

David Godwin carried out research in 2012 in Australia, over a decade later than Brierley. He writes: "as many as 50% of children raised in churches leave during this transition phase, which means that churches are losing more people at this time than at any other stage in the lifespan".[13]

Much of the research that has been done in the past decades reaches the same conclusion: the key years are between ages seven to ten where children are deciding if church is for them. As a children's pastor this should be a wake-up call! We can't leave the transition of children from primary to secondary school to the youth pastor as the children have already left by then!

So what can we do differently to ensure that half our kids aren't lost? What strategies can we put in place to transition well? I have been running a children's club for over three years and we are *intentional* about helping our Year 6s' transition to our youth programme. Goodwin's research showed that 80 per cent of churches do not plan for the transition of their children to youth or to adult church.

Over the last three years we have developed, and still are developing, a transition programme. Before starting any transition programme, find a transition team and pray! A transition team could be the children and youth pastor, volunteers from your children's group, youth group, parents of those in Year 6 (ages ten to eleven), or anyone with a heart for transition. Pray and get a vision; share your vision with the rest of your church. Below is an example of our transition plan for the UK (feel free to adapt for your context).

---

12   See www.christian-research.org/
13   Goodwin, David, *Lost in Transition*, Richmond: Kidsreach Publishing, 2013, p. 13.

TRANSITION TABLE	
Sep–March	Year 6 Socials (with Youth Leaders)
March	JR Leader Bootcamp at Kids Club
Easter	Year 6 Graduation Transition Packs sent to all Year 6 parents JR Leader training event
After Easter	JR Leaders at Kids Club & Join Youth Programme
May–Sep	Life Groups
June–July	Secondary School Party

Year 6 socials – Friends, food and fun are extremely important to this age group. With this in mind we always begin our Year 6 transition programme with a range of socials that will appeal to any member of this year group! We write to all the Year 6 parents explaining that we want to be able support their children in this period of change and provide a place where they can hang out and form friendships that they can take into Year 7. We try to give a wide range of socials such as bowling (followed by McDonalds), snowtubing, laser tag, a pool party, film nights, etc. It is really important that some of your youth team attend so that they can start to build relationships with the Year 6s!

Junior leader at Children's Club/Children's Church – Brierley's research showed that ten and eleven-year-olds want to help others – he found 62 per cent of tweenagers engaged in activities that helped others where they lived.[14] My experience has been that at our children's club, Years 5 and 6 feel too old for the club or "children's church" but they love being a leader. We specifically run a junior leaders' boot camp for our Year 6s straight after the February half-term. This is a time where they join the team and are trained over the course of a month. They can be trained in tech, dance, upfront team, or stage management, etc. by

---

14   Brierley, P., *Reaching and Keeping Tweenagers*, London: Christian Research Organisation, 2002.

our adult team. We then have a graduation ceremony before the Easter holidays and then the Year 6s become official members of the team. We don't want our Year 6 junior leaders (and the rest!) to feel they are being used but feel we are investing in them. In order to do this, we run junior leader socials and have team pastors who are responsible for their spiritual/pastoral development. Alongside this we are keen to build genuine relationships between the junior leaders and adult team.

Transition to youth group – So when is the best time to transition from the children's club/Sunday school to the youth club/youth church? I have found that straight after Easter is a good time and moving early means that they are not doing all the change stuff at the same time. We give our Year 6s the choice so they can attend both the children's club (as a junior leader or not) and the youth programme. In order to help with this we ask the youth team to attend our children's club just before the Easter break.

We also send out transition packs to every Year 6 parent, which consists of the following:

- letter and any flyers from the youth pastor, promoting the youth activities
- letter from the children's pastor promoting junior leader activities
- "It's Your Move" booklet – available from www.scriptureunion.org.uk.

Life groups – At Easter we encourage our Year 6s to join a life group – either an existing one or sometimes we have formed a Year-6 only group. Life groups for Year 6s (and upwards) are a great forum for allowing space and questions. Goodwin found that loss of faith or belief is a factor for 76 per cent of children who leave the church.[15] Research shows that children's thinking undergoes a shift which has an impact on the way they make moral and spiritual choices. Life groups or assigning spiritual mentors can be a place where they can study the Bible together and real engagement can take place.

Connecting with families – Brierley's research showed that tweenagers follow their parents' example when it comes to church

---

15   Goodwin, *Lost in Transition*, p.13.

attendance.[16] If this is the case then in our transition programme we also need to be reaching out to families. We regularly run family events through our kids' club so our non-church parents can build a trust with us. In our transition programme we have recently started to run transition workshops with our Year 6 parents (this has been done through our links with the school). We finish the Year 6 year with a "secondary school" party so that children and parents can meet before they start Year 7.

All of the above strategies rely on a good relationship between the children and youth teams. We have had a great success rate of seeing our children transition from our kids' club to our youth group. However, our Sunday kids and youth ministry is still a challenge, despite using similar transition strategies. Krish Kandiah, on behalf of the Evangelical Alliance, suggests that rather than giving the youth [or children's] worker the responsibility of keep the young people in church, it is "intergenerational churches that might keep more young people and foster an environment in which they can transition into adulthood rather than churches which keep children's work and youth ministry isolated from the main life of the church".[17]

Goodwin's research found that children who attend all or part of the adult service on a regular basis are twice as likely to make a successful transition to adult church.[18] Both Brierley and Goodwin's research suggests that tweenagers are not necessarily against the Christian faith but rather it is the church that they find it difficult to relate to. In the transition between primary and secondary, church becomes less important and relevant. Tweenagers are spiritual beings, but in order to grow in faith they need to be engaged and challenged and know that church is a community to belong to.

Kandiah raises an important issue and intergenerational ministry is something which needs to be included when looking at strategies on how to do transition well. In his article, Kandiah suggests ways that his local church have been experimenting with, such as helping rotas and mentoring during the church service. Tammy Tolman looks at what the environment would be like if ministry to children was within a

---

16   Brierley, *Reaching and Keeping Tweenagers*.
17   Krish Kandiah Blog, "It Takes a Whole Church…", February 2012: https://krishk. com/2012/02/takes-church/
18   Goodwin, *Lost in Transition*, p. 28.

healthy intergenerational community. She argues that this can be truly transformational, not only to the child, but also the family and the wider community.[19]

Working with tweenagers can be challenging but highly rewarding. Let's take the time to work out how we can effectively grow and nurture new generations of young people who love God and want to serve him through their whole lives. What can we do differently to ensure that half our kids aren't lost forever?

---

19   Tammy Tolman, *Collide: Exploring INTERGenerational Ministry*, NSW: Figtree, 2013.

The Third Dimension – Child Evangelism

So far we have two primary areas for the communication of faith: the immediate family and the faith community, and both are to impart spiritual knowledge and transmit living faith.

And that works. With varying degrees of success it travels through most of history. In Jesus' time, this was the pattern being outworked. The early Christians simply adopted the pattern. It's a powerful system instituted by God to help us keep God at the centre of our lives and enable us to communicate Him to the next generation. It is certainly very powerful, but it is also very fragile. If one generation misses it, the next is in jeopardy. If two miss it, serious cracks begin to appear. In much of the world over the last fifty years we have relied on the grandparent factor – simply stated, it wasn't the parents who brought their children up, but the grandparents – who saw faith as being of vital importance. This cushion disguised the crisis for some time, but in many countries we are now three generations away from the Jesus story in most homes.

The system has broken. But the important thing to realize is that we have been here before. In Britain in the 1700s, in a time of great social upheaval, the church was seriously caught out. Because of huge people movements and population increase, we found ourselves in a position where one parish church could be charged with attempting to serve a local population of 200,000 people (this was the case in Nottingham and Sheffield)! Nevertheless, despite large populations, churches remained empty. In speaking of the children of that time, the writers of the day stated that church was a place in which neither the children nor their ancestors had ever set foot. At least three generations removed.

תֵּיב

(Bah'ith)

הָחָפְּשָׁמ

(Mish-paw-khaw')

Child Evangelism

The pattern was broken and what was needed was a repair strategy. And that's why we needed a third dimension – the dimension of "child evangelism" – a strategy to engage with boys and girls whose parents will not bring them to church. Child evangelism can be simply defined as the communication of the Jesus story to boys and girls who wouldn't hear that story in any other way. And so in 1780 the Sunday school movement was born. By 1788, 300,000 boys and girls were attending these early children's projects; children primarily from non-church homes. By 1830 the adult population of church in Britain had doubled as a result of children growing up and joining the churches that had nurtured them. By 1904 85 per cent of British boys and girls were attached to church and church groups.

But don't misunderstand this. Child evangelism is a repair strategy, it is not the pattern; it is there to fix the pattern. Allow me to explain this by the only way I know how – another story.

John lives several doors down from the church. His parents never come to church, but from the age of seven they send John to your children's club, and John really likes it. You try all sorts of interesting and creative ideas to draw in John's parents, but they are not coming! John, however, keeps attending. Susie lives about a mile away. Mum brings her every week. Well, more accurately, drops her off at the door. Mum is a single mum and she likes the children's club because it gives her some much-needed time to herself. She's been to the church a few times, but says it's not for her. But Susie comes. Susie is also seven. Susie didn't like it at first, but Mum brought her anyway! Fortunately now she does like it. The years go by and both children move from children's club to youth group, and they've also started attending Sunday church. When they are in their mid-twenties they start to hold hands (twenty-five obviously being the appropriate age for holding hands!) and eventually they marry and have children of their own.

So the big questions. How did we reach John and Susie with the Jesus story? Through child evangelism. We communicated the Jesus story to two children who wouldn't have heard the Jesus story in any other way. But what about John and Susie's children? Do we need child evangelism there? No! Their children will hear about Jesus, the God who does things, in the context of *bah'ith*, at the kitchen table, from John and Susie, and every member of their church; their *mish-paw-khaw* will be communicating to them.

The children who are reached; who join our churches; who grow up in our churches, need to understand that their children will be nurtured in the captivating Jesus story in the context of *bah'ith* (in their own homes) and in *mish-paw-khaw* (their local church) – they don't need child evangelism. We need child evangelism as a priority at this point in history, but we should believe for the time when all children can be nurtured in the context of *bah'ith* and *mish-paw-khaw*. All it would take would be for us to reach one whole generation.

Allow me to repeat that last part – **this whole thing takes three generations to break, but only one to repair.**

But the key is this: at this point in history we need all three dimensions in our local church children's ministries. We need to work in all three areas, publish in all three areas, and teach about all three areas. If you are a children's worker and part of the team, you may get the luxury of choosing which dimension to specialize in. If you are a church leader or leader of your kids' ministry, you don't get that luxury. At this point in history our children's ministry must be in three dimensions.

Robert Raikes Legacy

"The character of many of the youngsters was transformed. Their swearing, rudeness, and unruliness was replaced by a sense of duty."[20]

The quote above refers to something that happened nearly 300 years ago. It isn't describing a new police initiative or government reform, it is something more radical than that. The transformation in question was the result of Sunday school attendance. The institution of Sunday school stretches way back in history. The first recorded Sunday schools began in 1756, but their establishment took on more momentum in the hands of Robert Raikes, the editor of *The Gloucester Journal*. In this day of rising crime, particularly among the young, there is another interesting by-product of Sunday school: as Sunday school attendance increased, the crime rate in Raikes' city and county dropped sharply. At the Easter Quarter Sessions of 1786, the magistrates passed a unanimous vote of thanks for the benefits of Sunday schools for the morals of the young. This is what evangelism does; it connects all the partners up – local government, various churches, judicial services – and leads all forward to a place of community transformation.

This is one of the most exciting times to be alive if you have even the slightest hint of an evangelistic spirit within you. I often hear how terrible things are today. How children when asked about Easter or Christmas answer with stories of eggs, bunnies and trees. There was a story once told about two salesmen who were sent to ply their trade on an island where nobody wore shoes. The two salesmen arrived and walked in two different directions, agreeing to meet back at the harbour in a month's time. When they returned the first had sold nothing and was despondent: "This is useless, nobody wears shoes here." The second had sold his entire stock: "This is wonderful, nobody

20   Christian History Institute, *Children's Heroes from Christian History*, Vol. 2, www.visionvideo.com/files/ChHeroesChrHist2guide.pdf.

wears shoes." It's a matter of perspective. We either shake our heads in despair because so many families don't know Jesus, or we get excited by the possibilities in front of us.

Let me unpack this further. If this were a century ago and you needed to immunize someone against smallpox, you would most likely give them contact to cowpox. Cowpox would be hardly noticeable, but the effect of being exposed to cowpox would cause the body to build up the necessary antibodies to immunize the individual against smallpox. What we have done, in effect, is given people something like it, that has the effect of immunizing them against it. That's pretty much what we have done with the Jesus story in many places for over fifty years. We have presented something like Jesus, but it is a presentation that is without power: God who is passive, a God who cannot transform. It's why so many people have a negative view of Sunday school. A boring, tedious afternoon's activity that they couldn't wait to escape. And parents and grandparents who attended a children's programme like that don't send their children and grandchildren to our provisions. We immunized them against the Jesus story. But what happens when you are three generations removed from the Jesus story in most homes in a particular country? The immunization effect has worn off. We once again have an entire generation ready to receive the glorious, life-transforming Jesus story.

This means that you and I get to paint on a blank canvas, presenting the Jesus story to entire families who have never heard the Jesus story before. But what is important is that we paint in primary colours. Tell the whole Jesus story. The Jesus who was born into abject poverty for them, who lived a sinless life, always speaking truth, the Jesus who died a painful horrific death, feeling forsaken. The Jesus who rose again. Defeating death. The Jesus who sits at the right of the Father praying for us. We tell the whole story because there are people who need to hear that Jesus loved them so much that he left heaven for them. There are those who need to know that Jesus felt hurt and forsaken because they feel hurt and forsaken too. But the Jesus who overcame death, through the resurrection, showed that everything is possible.

Re-evangelization is possible. There is something in that incredible pattern of child evangelism modelled by Raikes many centuries ago that you and I can take hold of now and use to create the most exciting child evangelism projects today. The following pages will look more closely at those elements as we discuss how to start and run an outreach children's club – child evangelism on the ground.

The Raikes Elements

The following chapters will look more closely at those elements that need to be in place to establish exceptional children's outreach projects. Elements that were present several centuries ago when Raikes developed children's outreach projects to reach 300,000 boys and girls within eight years of inception (in those days, children's outreach took the form of Sunday schools only[21]).

There is nothing clever here, but the omission of any of the elements outlined will negatively impact the overall effectiveness of these outreach projects. It will come as no surprise, therefore, that the first element to be included involves "people". It will always stand or fall on the people who run the outreach. But there are more subtle elements – the connection between the outreach project and the local church for example.

But don't lose sight of what these elements can do. In just eight years, 300,000 children from primarily non-churched homes reached. That's more children than are in church in the UK every Sunday today. These elements will not give you staggering adult attendance by the end of the year, but they will enable you to grow a church from children upwards over the next few decades.

Professional teachers

We have already visited the first Sunday school teachers in looking at the area of misconceptions and at Mrs Critchley, the force of nature who led the very first Sunday school. And at that point in history, "professional" really did mean paid to do it. But I want to give this word "professional" a far wider definition and say that "professional" means "doing it properly". The definition is probably shown well in the example of Mr Nisbet, one of the founder members of the Sunday School Union, who would rise at 4 a.m. to study the necessary chapters

---

21   For a comprehensive overview of this check out my book *One Generation from Extinction*, Oxford: Monarch Books, 2009.

that had been appointed as the lessons for the next Sunday, aiding his study with reference to Matthew Henry's commentary! And while I am not advocating this particular commentary, I am advocating this level of commitment. Why 4 a.m.? Because Mr Nisbet would be working the other six days of the week and this would be his only opportunity to prepare properly. And while the stories of people teaching Sunday school while still drunk that we see in the chronicles of the nineteenth and early twentieth-century Sunday school are hopefully in the past, we still have too many children's workers who roll out bed on a Sunday, realize that they are on the roster for that day and stumble in, ill prepared. And what do they do? They immunize another generation against the compelling, captivating Jesus story. We must do this properly.

It is without doubt that your ability to reproduce leaders will be **the single most important factor** that will determine the extent of your vision. When children's workers have been asked to write down what topics they would like covered in seminars, this one always comes up: "How do I get more leaders?" In many ways it is not about how well we run the race, it is about how many people we get running. So how do we do it? How do we develop leaders?

Be a leader

There has been much talk in recent years about the role of leaders in the church context. I believe in the plurality of leadership. I am a huge supporter of the whole congregation rising up and fulfilling their role in the body of Christ. But I am also a passionate believer in God-given leadership. From the dawn of time until the end of time God insists on raising up individuals who will bring clear direction to his people. Be that kind of leader. **Lead with compassion, conviction and courage and people will follow you.** Lead by democratic committee and change your views according to popular consent and you are going nowhere.

But a few more keys to leading well:

We must start with a vision

Proverbs 29:18 tells us, "Where there is no vision, the people perish" (KJV). The applications for this verse are numerous. Clearly in its context it is talking about a vision of God. But the principle can allow a wider application. If people have nothing to aim for, nothing to run after, nothing that consumes and motivates them, then they will:

- stumble all over themselves (*The Message*)
- cast off restraint (NKJ)
- run wild (NLT)
- perish (KJV).

People need something to pursue. Sir Ernest Shackleton, the famous explorer, once placed an advertisement in a newspaper in 1900:

MEN WANTED FOR HAZARDOUS ADVENTURE

Small wages, long months of complete darkness, constant danger. Safe return doubtful. Honour and recognition in case of success.

He commented that it seemed half of England had responded to the advert. People want something to give their lives for. Visionary people often attract a following. People will come with you if they know that you are going somewhere. We recruit to a vision, and never simply ask for volunteers. When Jesus approached the disciples he said, "Follow me and I will make you fishers of men" (Matthew 4:19, RSV). He was recruiting to a vision.

You cannot, and must not, recruit to desperation. Calls for help that begin, "We are desperate for help, if you don't help we will have to stop/close", are never likely to cause people to come running. Vocalize vision: "There is an opportunity to be involved in one of the most exciting things this church does..." may just get you the people you need. But don't just state it, publish it. Habakkuk 2:2 says, "Write this. Write what you see. Write it out in big block letters so that it can be read on the run" (*The Message*). It is often not until the vision is actually written down that it can begin to be outworked. Writing it down means that the visionary mind has to put into words what it has seen and felt and perceived. This is an important part of the process. It needs to be easily understood and as God's instruction to Habakkuk points out, it needs to be clear. This is particularly important as the next stage is to share it with others. Now begin to share it with a small group. Jesus' message would change the world, but to get that message around the world he started with a small group and poured his life into them. Often they missed it, often they completely misunderstood what the prime directive was, but he continued to pour himself into this group. We need to learn from this. If we can share the vision with six to twelve people and do so in such a way that they begin to own the vision as their own, then they in turn will gather people around themselves, and so the vision begins to spread. And then we are up and running. We have an inner core of leaders who will share the message with the next level of leaders and so on. And finally, keep recruiting. 1 Samuel 14:52 gives us an insight into King Saul at his best: "So whenever Saul observed a young man who was brave and strong, he drafted him into his army" (NLT).

King Saul's philosophy was simple – constant recruitment. When I spend my summers taking children's camps, or when I travel around the country taking leadership development sessions, I am not averse to seeing a person who clearly has the hand of God on their life and inviting them to come and work with me. It is the King Saul philosophy. The philosophy has another attribute. It means we don't make the mistake of trying to fill positions. King Saul was not about filling positions; he was about bringing people of character on board. These sorts of people will create their own position; just get them on board.

Once your leaders have captured your heart then allow them to recruit as well. Allow them to form their own teams under them. They are all still outworking the vision that you presented to them, but now they own it. Don't get upset if it looks a little different to what you intended. Keep your eye on the end goal. If you are still on course for the end goal, then be secure enough to allow your leaders some room for interpretation of the vision as they begin to mature and develop.

In summary, we recruit to a vision by:

- vocalizing it
- writing it down
- gathering a small group/team
- continuing to recruiting
- getting our leaders recruiting.

Leaders tend to fall into four categories:

+	Leaders who add to what you are doing. Keep them, they are a blessing, but work with them; they may be able to do more than that.
–	Leaders who subtract from what you are doing. Those who drop the drinks tray in the middle of your appeal. Those who can't seem to make it to meetings on time. Work with these. Ultimately they may have to step down, but not before we invest enough time and energy and prayer in them to be able to say we did our best.
X	Leaders who multiply what you do. Those who everything they touch turns to gold. Those who can take on the failing project and make it happen. These people are like gold. Never take them for granted.
÷	Leaders who are divisive; leaders who undermine. This one is very simple. You ask them to leave as quickly as possible. Don't entertain them. Don't allow them to compromise what God is doing. This may seem cold, but it is so important. If I have made a major mistake in ministry, it is keeping divisive people around too long. Nail it early.

Set standards for your workers

There are some basics that must be present in your workers' lives. Remember, these leaders will be the examples that the children look to in order to model their lives. They must have a genuine relationship with God, read their Bibles and pray regularly, and lives that reflect Christian values, have a sense of fun and life, and a willingness to be teachable. In all this there are still important issues regarding who we recruit as leaders. I have been horrified by the number of stories I have heard recently of paedophiles targeting churches. Most countries now have statutory checks for everyone who works with children. Be diligent in this area. It is exceptionally important. But even with a clear check in place, I never allow a person to be alone with a child or group of children. My groups are always taught by at least two people. We can no longer blindly trust people.

Training is vital

Your leaders are like gold – without them the impact of the vision will be greatly diminished. So ensure that they always have they opportunity for training. Most countries now have exceptional training for children and family workers – training on everything from puppet ministry, to storytelling, to worship and ministry in the power of the Spirit. But don't just send them for training or host your own training, always pay for your workers to go on training courses. Always. Jesus said, "Where your treasure is, there will your heart be also" (Matthew 6:21, RSV). When we pay for our leaders to attend training events we shout loudly and clearly that our heart is in this area. And I'd would be keen to take this one stage further. Don't just send your leaders on training days, pay for them to go on children and family ministry training retreats. They need to be able to listen, and then earth those ideas with other children and family workers. They need to draw strength and encouragement from others doing what they are doing. It really isn't an optional extra.

> TIP: THE TEAM T-SHIRT is far more important that you realize. Particularly for a young team. Place all your young team in T-shirts of the same colour with your club or church logo. Those who graduate to become the older team can choose different colours. You'll see the young team want to graduate to be the older team, but you'll also notice quickly that your younger children aspire to become the young team and thus get to wear the T-shirt.

And now I will give you *the key* to leadership development. The key to ensuring that you always have a strong leadership base for many years to come. Are you ready? The heading won't fill you with hope, but here you go, introducing:

The most useless category of leader

A bit of narrative:

> It's a New Wine summer festival. There are thousands of children on site: 600 of them in the venue for three and four-year-olds. And because we need a huge number of volunteers we often have

thirteen-year-old boys as junior leaders for small groups of three or four-year-olds in this venue. I may offend you with this, but I've been around a while. I promise you that thirteen-year-old boys are the most useless category of leader it is possible to have. They can barely walk properly, they drip hormones as they walk and they are always late.

It's Monday morning, the children have just been dropped off. The worship time is about to begin. I pop in to see how everyone is getting on when the thirteen-year-old boy comes bobbing towards me. He boldly announces, "I need to go and get one of the mums, one of my four-year-old girls is not well. Can I go?"

I ask the usual question, "Does God do stuff? Is He for real?"

He looks a little uncomfortable at being asked such a tricky question. He stares at his shoes. I help him, "Yes He does. So what I need you to do is going back and pray for her."

He looks worried, but he walks back towards his group. He only gets halfway when he turns and comes back. He looks at me quite concerned and admits, "I don't know what to say."

I help him with some words, "God make her better. Amen."

I watch as he walks back repeating the words of the prayer over and over...

He kneels, he prays and then like a shot he is back with me, "I did it, now can I get her mum or dad?"

I put my arm on his shoulder. And walk him back over to his group. I kneel beside the little girl and I say, "Hi, my name is Mark. Who are you?"

"Zoe," comes the response.

"And what just happened Zoe?"

And she looks at thirteen-year-old boy with big wide eyes. Because herein lies one of the mysteries of the universe. I may think thirteen-year-old boys are the most useless category of leader, but four-year-old girls love them! She says, "He prayed for me because my tummy was poorly."

And then I ask her, "And what happened?"

She smiles. "My tummy got better."

And suddenly it's the turn of the thirteen-year-old boy to have wide eyes. He can't believe it. The words that he'd heard since he was a toddler are true. The great God of the universe is real and just worked through him. He is so excited. He just moved from being yet another consumer attached to church to being a producer or, to use another word, a disciple. And of course he's now a nightmare. I have produced a healing evangelist and now he wants to pray for everyone in his venue and anyone else he can find. He's wandering around asking people if they are unwell because if they are, he can pray. I'm sure he will be on a God Channel near you at some point in the future.

I know recruiting so young is loaded with difficulty; I know most of them have no concept of responsibility, I know that most of them fall in the minus ("–") leadership category (they detract from what we do). They are hard work. But if we can carry them through the first couple of years, they are only useless for a year. By age fourteen you begin to see what incredible leaders you are producing. By age sixteen you have leaders of excellence. And they never ever turn around and say, "We've never done it this way before." They know how you think, and how you work. They came through your children's programmes, they know what you do, and they are living proof that it works. They will still mess up. They will still be easily distracted and turn up late for your meetings because the boy/girl down the street needed to talk to them, but they are worth the investment. It may even be worthwhile having a monthly discipleship/training meeting just for your younger leaders, depending on how many you can recruit.

Are we looking for brilliant teachers who can set the world on fire with the oratory gifts? Not necessarily. But our ability to develop *professional* leaders is critical to what we are trying to do. But allow me to re-emphasize the main point here with a story borrowed from the amazing Max Lucado:

John Blanchard was a lieutenant in the Second World War. His hobby was reading books. Whenever he had free time John would sneak off to the library. On this particular day he had gone to the library and picked up a book bound in light blue material from the shelf. He began to read but was distracted by the comments that had been written in the margins of the book by someone who he guessed was the book's previous owner. Sure enough at the end of the book was the name and address of the previous owner, one Hollis Maynell, who lived in New York City. He wrote to her and simply said that he enjoyed her comments. She wrote back. One year and one month of writing then took place and the two formed a loving relationship within these letters. But no matter how many times John asked Hollis refused to send him a photograph. He was drafted overseas, but still the letters continued. Eventually he returned to the United States and they arranged to meet. The time was set – 7 p.m., and the place – Grand Central Station. She would wear a rose and he would wear his best dress uniform.

He arrived at the station as the clock struck 7 p.m. People began to leave the train that had just pulled in. And as he gazed, a lady started walking towards him; her figure was long and slim. Her blonde hair lay back in curls from her delicate ears; her eyes were as blue as flowers. Her lips and chin had a gentle firmness, and in her pale green suit she looked like springtime come alive.

John moved towards her but entirely forgetting to notice that she was not wearing a rose. As he got closer, a small provocative smile curved her lips and she whispered, "Going my way, sailor?"

Almost uncontrollably John made one step closer to her, and then he saw Hollis Maynell. She was standing almost directly behind the girl. She was a woman well past 40, she had greying hair tucked under a hat. She was more than plump and her thick-ankled feet were thrust into low-heeled shoes.

The girl in the pale green suit was quickly walking away. John was torn. What should he do? So keen was his desire to follow her and yet so deep was his longing for the woman whose spirit had truly companioned and upheld his own. And there she stood. Her pale, plump face was gentle and sensible; her grey eyes had a warm and kindly twinkle. John didn't hesitate. He squared his shoulders and saluted, "I am Lt John Blanchard. I am so glad you could meet me. May I take you to dinner?"

The woman's face broadened into a tolerant smile. She said, "I don't know what this is about, son. But that young lady in the green suit who just went by, she begged me to wear this rose on my coat. And she said if you ask me to dinner, I should tell you she is waiting in the big restaurant across the street. She said it was some kind of test!"[22]

Hollis Maynell knew that she wanted to be with someone who was prepared to look deeper than a pretty face. This was about more than

---

22   Lucado, Max, *And the Angels Were Silent*, Thomas Nelson Publishers, 1992.

appearance, this was about the heart.

And therein lies the key to this chapter. We may not find the most qualified leaders, we may never find the most gifted leaders, but if we can find people who love children and whose hearts are right then we will never go far wrong. Skills and procedures we can teach, the right heart spirit is something the person must arrive with.

Don't try and build with people who look good, build with people who have the right heart. They may not have a burden for children's work, they can get that from you, they might not understand the practical implications, they can get that from you as well. But a teachable spirit and a right heart are foundation stones.

God spends his time looking for a builder whose heart is right. God is not worried about what will be built, for if the heart of the builder is right then the building will be just fine. God is looking for "wise master builders" (1 Corinthians 3:10) and that title is given to people whose heart is right.

Connection with church

An important element is the connection with the church. How does your outreach project connect to the local church? There are a lot of ways of making connections between the family and children's outreach ministry, ranging from "No kids" on one end of the pendulum to "Integrated" on the other. Let's take a look:

No kids

Clearly this represents there being no connection with children and families. And there is a caution here. Most denominations have been very keen to promote children, family and youth ministry across their regions/areas/diocese and they have made a particular effort to target churches that have no children. But they have often done this without asking the fundamental question – do the members of that church want children in their church and in their services? The reality is that children are not always quite well behaved and skilled at outworking a mantra of being seen and not heard. In one church I visited, a previous vicar had insisted that any children who attended remove their shoes so they couldn't kick the pews. They didn't need to be asked for too long, they felt so unwanted they never returned anyway, but curiously those messages embed themselves in communities and several ministers later they were still struggling to get children to return.

Children can certainly disrupt liturgy, do unpredictable things in the talk time, and don't have a great reputation for maintaining silence. And the simple reality is that some congregations would prefer to have services without children. They like their style and form of worship and they don't want it disrupted. Curiously I have no issue with that. It's honest and clear. The issue for me comes from churches that pretend they want more young families when everything they do says they are not prepared to be in any way accommodating.

The solution for me is simple enough. We need to stop throwing energy and resources at these sort of churches in an attempt to encourage children and family attendance. Let's use our energies in churches that are interested and will be welcoming and accommodating. The other type will eventually die out and then we can plant a new church with a different ethos into their building. But there is no urgency, there are plenty of available places to plant at the moment.

Para church groups

This is when other groups will come in and run a children's and family activity for you. This is a really helpful and useful thing if it is pitched properly. Whether it is a child evangelism fellowship beach mission, or a Scripture Union summer camp, both are clearly valuable. But if it is a mission organization that you have parachuted in to run a range of outreach activities for you for a period, then this can go one of two ways. If they have come to kickstart a ministry that you have been preparing to launch for some time, and you plan to continue that ministry, then this is a useful tool. If you want a group to come in and envision your church to go and engage in children, youth and family ministry then this is also valuable – which is a good thing since I have spent a lot of time doing a lot of this over many decades of ministry.

But if the local church is bringing a group in to do it *instead of* you, then it is not going to end well. They will create a local church boom and bust event. The flatness felt by local church and by the wider community when the group leaves will create a climate of despondency that will be hard to shift.

It is better to do a lesser thing but locally owned and initiated than to parachute outside ministries in. We mustn't get caught in the trap of the quick fix.

Bolt-on ministry

"When do you run your holiday club?"
"First week of the summer holidays."
"Why?"
"To get it out of the way."

And there is my clue showing that we are dealing with a bolt-on ministry. Many churches feel guilty if they do not run a family outreach event or a children's mission activity in the course of the year. It's not necessarily who they are, and it doesn't necessarily flow from the heart of the church membership. But they know they should be doing something, so they do. It's difficult to address because there are likely to be some well-meaning people behind these sorts of events who have been the driving force for many decades. But they take huge effort and often huge resources in terms of people. But their long-term effectiveness is limited. Surely little and often is better.

Bridge ministries

"Why are we doing all these community activities for children and families and teenagers? They are not making Sunday attendance any larger. We need to focus on Sunday. That's the most important." This is a statement I heard from an Anglican church warden recently. It belies an interesting perspective which basically believes that only Sunday ministry is proper church and everything else we do is a bridge to Sunday. And of course bridge ministries are important and valuable. It could be argued that all sorts of things are *bridge* activities – from Alpha to community fireworks. The issue is this: if the bridge doesn't work, if nobody makes that walk across it into Sunday, does it still have validity? Is it still something we should be doing? Is it still important? If the only purpose of Messy Church, or the Children's Club, or our ministry into schools, is to see increased attendance on Sunday, then I would dare to suggest that we have missed the point.

These ministries have value in their own right. I suspect the recognition of that will bring to an end the ever-present question of, "Is Messy Church working when they are not coming to church?" If you read Rachel Hill-Brown's article on Messy Church later on in this section you will see clearly that her version of Messy Church *is* church. She is pastoring them, seeing them come to Jesus and discipling them in small groups. Sounds like church to me. In the next section you will also see my heartfelt plea for more examples of children's outreach as a way of church planting, a way of seeing an intergenerational church develop. Literally, growing a church.

Connecting with schools

The 2001 Dearing Report[23] is a Church of England document that put simply encourages church schools to behave like church schools, and asks the local church to see the school as a place of mission on the same level as the church. Not only is this bold, but it may also have a stronger integrity. It is not advocating a model that uses the school to attract people to the church; instead, it is a model that recognizes the significance of the school as a place of mission. When I was a senior minister in the south of England I made a point of planting churches into local schools. It was an exceptionally successful way of connecting with local communities: putting local congregations close to the communities and locating a church within walking distance of large numbers of people. But Dearing is suggesting more than that. Our local church school conducted acts of collective worship every day (the terminology is important – not "assemblies" but "collective worship"); the Friday also involved parents. Intergenerational family worship in the school. What a wonderful opportunity. We are talking about church schools where there are also opportunities to base prayer corners in each classroom so children can think further about what they encountered in collective worship. All church schools should be like this. And while I know the international picture has different nuances, schools connected to churches really should be "church schools" centres of mission in their own right.

---

23   www.churchofengland.org/media/1118777/way%20ahead%20-%20whole.pdf

Integrated

Peter Brierley said to me once:

> All growing churches have an effective children's ministry. And they deliberately see that ministry as part of the mainstream activity of the church. This integration mechanism of the children's ministry with the totality of the church activity is as important as the quality of the actual ministry itself if growth is to take place.[24]

Children's ministry has to be at the heart of everything we do. And therefore the simple reality is that it must be in the heart of the senior leader. If your senior leader doesn't have a heart for family ministry and you do, then you really only have two choices: pray and pray and pray that God will change his heart; or pack your gifts, skills and talents into your bag and set off for the next part of your adventure with God. If one of these two things doesn't happen then you will constantly feel frustrated.

When I became a senior minister, in the first couple of weeks I made this statement:

> If there is ever a time when we don't have enough leaders to be with our children on a Sunday morning, I'm not going to preach to you, I'm going to pop to the church hall and preach to them. You see I've read the statistics. If you are thirty years of age and over and still in church, then it is likely that you are staying forever. But up until the age of thirty we are losing boys and girls and young adults at such a rate that if I don't focus on them, we'll have no church half a century from now.

Fortunately most of them got it. And I do believe it. But what it did over and above the words is it placed our ministry to children, young people and families at the very heart of what we do.

So as this section comes to an end, let's earth all that. Bearing in mind the above, draw your present set-up. Does anything need a rethink?

---

24   In a personal letter to me.

Your church set-up in picture form

Connection with the community

We have to learn afresh to engage with communities. The transformation of all human life under God ought to be the goal. Working with local government to see the communities transformed should be the norm. The idea of *us* inside the walls of our church buildings and *them* outside is a long way from the model that Jesus presented. In fact whenever you see *them* and *us* thinking, you know that we've strayed from the Jesus model of ministry. To illustrate the point allow me to tell you a story of an event in a parish I was part of a few years ago:

> I was working with a smallish church. We'd done some work with the youth of the area and were seeing quite a lot of them attending our Friday night event. I was approaching the point where I would be moving on and they really needed a specialist youth worker. I approached the church council who agreed completely that we needed a youth worker, but they didn't think we could go down that route because there wasn't enough money in the budget. This wasn't a surprising response. But I clarified the situation. If we did have the money you would like a youth worker? It's always useful to make things clear. They did.
>
> The following week I went to see the local parish council (for our international readers, that's the group of local government with limited responsibilities, and fairly limited budget – fairly limited, because I knew that this particular council had money set aside for youth work and had it set aside for quite some time – local knowledge is always useful). I got to the council meeting early and asked the chairperson if members of the public, i.e., me, were allowed to ask things. They informed me that members of the public were given the first fifteen minutes of the meeting to ask questions, but that fifteen minutes would have to be split between all the people who came. Since I was the only one I wasn't sure that would be a problem. When it came time for my question I asked, "I would like you to fund a community youth worker that the church will line manage."
>
> They laughed. I didn't. They eventually realized I was serious and then came the question, "Why should we give this money to you? This money is for the community, not the church."
>
> And I could see it clearly. I said to them, "The difficulty you're having is that you've fallen into the trap of them and us thinking,

it's not about church and council and community, it's about some of us who are called to service all of us. If you and I work together we can do some significant good in this community."

At least they'd stopped laughing. There were some mutters and then they asked me to leave the room for a few minutes. When I returned – I think more to their surprise than mine – they said that they were willing to fund a youth worker but they would need it to be a humanist youth worker and not a Christian one – they always get confused about these things so I helped them with a few more words, "That's very interesting and quite innovative. I've read the last census. And it suggests that 82 per cent of the area describe themselves as Christian. A further 9 per cent are Muslim, 4 per cent are Sikh, 2 per cent Hindu, 2 per cent are agnostic/atheist/humanist and the final 1 per cent are miscellaneous – apparently they are Jedi and the like! So, you would like to use community money to cater for the needs of 2 per cent of the population? Very innovative."

They asked me to leave the room again!

When I returned this time I was conscious that my fifteen minutes was now approaching the hour mark. But the local councillors were looking far more worn down than me. They quickly explained that they had made a mistake, "We didn't mean humanist, we meant inclusive. We need a youth worker who is inclusive."

I couldn't resist it, "You want someone who is inclusive, like Jesus was?"

They seemed to have lost the will to live, they simply nodded! So I summed up, "I will do my best to go and find a youth worker who is just like Jesus, that the church will line manage and you will pay for the next three years."

They nodded. They minuted it. And it happened.

And of course tied up with this is the problem that some churches and ministers will only consider community initiatives and involvement if ultimately they lead a path to church attendance. While I am very keen to propagate community activities that achieve this, I think if we are only involved in our communities and cities and towns for the purpose of winning people to our congregation then we have missed something very important. God called us to be salt and light. He called us to shine in dark places. We should work in our communities to make them better because we want our communities to be better. We should provide safe play environments because play is a good thing and safety is a good thing. We should support community initiatives even if they do not directly benefit us because they benefit our communities. We must move into a much more holistic view of what we do and why we do it.

Why does all this work? Because we refuse to operate under "them and us" thinking. Some of us are called to serve the rest of us. That's what community engagement looks like. The Anglican concept of the parish as an area where we can focus our attention is a good one. It needs some rethinking and the boundary should undoubtedly become a porous one, but self-restricting our work to a specific geographical area – whether it be the large "Ministry Areas" that the Church in Wales are experimenting with or the smaller parishes of the Church of England or the enormous parishes of the Australian church – it brings clarity and focus and allows vision to develop for a specific group (or groups) of people.

Because of this I have always had an ongoing dilemma with churches that send out buses to pick up children over a wide geographical area to bring them back to a central location. Invariably they will gather large crowds. I tried it myself for a season while working as a children's pastor in Milton Keynes. It took our numbers up to 750 children. But we were sending buses over 100 square miles to achieve this. I have seen similar activities in various parts of the country. We soon realized that we could gather hundreds of children each week with no buses and because they lived closer, the community impact was significantly increased (the most important factor). The model invariably comes from Bill Wilson's Metro Children's Club (part of Metro World Child) in New York. But a closer analysis of his work will reveal he doesn't send his buses more than two miles from the base, focusing on a small geographical area, albeit highly populated. Beyond two miles he switches to satellite outreach projects. In Bill's case those satellites are called Sidewalk Sunday School – converted vehicles with drop-down sides where events can be conducted in the open air.

What is also difficult about the bus ministry version of children's outreach is the cost. In the early twenty-first century some parts of the UK had children's outreach projects paying £50,000 and upwards to keep their buses on the road, while driving vast distances past numerous other churches to achieve their goal of large attendance. Many of them have now closed as they were not financially sustainable. The pattern British churches were following was an American one, the most famous advocate being the aforementioned Bill Wilson who had tens of thousands of attendees. A good example of the British church borrowing an American pattern and misunderstanding the application.

Meeting a social need

It is possible to institute social reform without a religious element, but it is impossible to provide any form of religious education devoid of a social element. We once had a very interesting child attend one of our after-school projects. He had been fostered and the foster parents were considering adoption. The only problem was the child was wild! We had just fitted a light blue carpet in the church hall (why light blue I will never know – I am beginning to suspect that church councils have no idea what church buildings are actually for). We had just started snacktime, which happened to involve tomato soup. He was enjoying splashing it everywhere. One of the leaders asked him to eat properly. He responded by throwing the tomato soup at the leader. Unfortunately, the leader managed to avoid the soup, which landed all over the new carpet (it would have been much easier to clean up the leader than to clean up the new carpet and explain to the church council what had happened). The options were clear. We could keep this child or ask him to leave the project. We knew a little of the background (the first five years of his life before social services rescued him could only be described as a living hell). We decided to keep the child. He was not from one of our church families. He didn't become a regular attendee at our children's club. But we chose to keep him. We later discovered that one of the main reasons that the family had chosen to adopt him and not return him to care was that we had chosen to keep him on in the after-school club. Has he become a member of the church? No. Has the family? No. Did we make a difference? Did we positively affect our community and our world? Absolutely! Did it make a difference to that little boy? Absolutely! You see the point; this is not about church attendance, this is about the Kingdom of God being manifest in an expression of love, joy and peace in the Holy Spirit. And in passing, two churches later when I was senior minister and got to make the choice, I opted for a stone floor. It was gorgeous. I also invested in some good mops.

There is so much involved in this area of meeting a social need. When Raikes started his Sunday schools there was a very real part to them that was interested in teaching boys and girls to read and write. But don't miss how powerful that is. The Enlightenment had taken place, modernism was on the rise, and arguably would peak there towards the back end of the eighteenth century. Modernism brought about a change in culture and in things that were valued. It brought a shift from that which was oral to that which is written. The written word became authoritative. And Raikes, as the editor of *The Gloucester Journal* was king of the written word. When he recognized the power of the written word he decided to give that power to local children. This is more than social reform, this is empowerment. He knew that without being able to write, those with fathers and grandfathers in the mill would also be going to work in the mill; those with relations in the coal mine would be going to work in the coal mine. There was no choice, no options. But if they could read and write they could be apprenticed to the solicitor or the accountant; they could work in new media; they could enter local government. He was empowering boys and girls. Hundreds of years later, modernism has lost its power. Postmodernism brought with it a move from that which is written to that which is oral. We no longer trust the written word, but once again we look to the gifted orator. The social currency has changed. But the task of empowering boys and girls continues. What would be the social currency in the village and towns and cities where you minister? What could you do to empower a new generation? The gospel itself allows boys and girls to become everything God created them to be and to see families transformed. But what is your part? On my journey I have run homework clubs, breakfast and after-school clubs for children of working parents and provided safe play opportunities because I recognize the formational importance of play. These activities don't always look spiritual, but if you are empowering your community, it is deeply spiritual.

Visiting

Like many firsts in children's ministry, the first home visits take place in the eighteenth century. Robert Raikes writes an account of his visit to a certain family. They had not sent their son to Sunday school that day and Raikes wanted to know why. It was soon explained to him that the child hadn't been sent because his weekend clothes were dirty, the weather had been dreadful, they couldn't wash them, and the parents did not want to send their child out with dirty clothes. Raikes responded simply, "All that I require is clean faces, clean hands, and hair combed, nothing more." You see, there were standards attached to the early Sunday schools, but they were standards that all could reach. Clean hands and face and combed hair. (We may struggle to enforce the third part of that today. There weren't a lot of messy-look hairstyles in Raikes' day.)

It would be easy to underestimate the significance of visiting. But I would go as far as to suggest that alongside schools work, visiting is the factor that ensures large attendance over a long period of time. Possibly the best way to explain how this all hangs together is to explain the procedures and practices from first attendance.

THE FIRST VISIT

When a child first attends the children's club they must come with a parent or guardian, or attend with a completed registration form. The registration form should contain at least the following information:

There are other items that can be added such as doctor's name, surgery address, etc.

**Children's Ministry
REGISTRATION FORM**

This form must be completed before your child attends one of our activities

Child's name: _____

Address: _____

_____

_____

Tel number:_____DoB:_____

Mobile number:

E-mail:

School Attended:

Medical conditions to be aware of:

_____

_____

In case of a major accident, your child will be taken, by ambulance if possible, to the nearest casualty department and parents will be informed as soon as possible. If this is not the procedure you would like us to follow for your child, please notify us in writing.

Signed:_____ Date:_____

Office Use: Team Colour:

Once the information has been given it should be filed according to child's address and the child's name added to the register. If you are using a computer package then the process becomes much easier. By putting the information into a computer program such as Microsoft Access™ then the user is able to retrieve the following:

• an updated register
• a list of children whose birthdays fall each week
• a printout of information sorted according to location of their house
• a list of children who are eligible to join the youth programme.

Someone who is computer literate will need to set up the appropriate templates that allow this information to be retrieved, but once it is up and running, inputting the information and accessing the necessary documents should be fairly straightforward.

There is of course a reason that the information is sorted into child's address. A couple of days before the next children's club it is useful to visit the children in their homes. If the children's club is large then the visits need to be divided between several people.

> TIP: Don't keep changing the person responsible for visiting a specific area. This is about forming relationships and parents learn to trust a certain face. If we want to build a relationship with the parents that allows open and honest discourse – firstly about the child but later about the gospel in general – then we need to keep the same person knocking on the same door week in week out.

Visits will take on many levels of contact. The visit may simply involve knocking on the door and handing over the colouring competition for the following week (see Appendix 4 for an example). As relationships develop it may involve popping in for a cup of tea and a chat. Because I can get away with it I tell the children that unless I get a biscuit when I knock on their door then I will not hand over the colouring competition – the children know I'm joking (actually it got embarrassing once when a parent came to the door to apologize that she hadn't been shopping yet and there were no biscuits left but could she still have the colouring competition?). The reverse of the colouring competition may be used to carry information about your club, but it may also carry information about your church services, counselling information, contact phone number for the minister, etc.

Visits achieve much:

- They give parents a chance to express concerns about the children's club. If they didn't get that chance to express concern then they may simply stop their child attending.
- They give you a chance to express any concerns about the child to the parent face to face.
- They allow relationship and trust to develop. In one study eight out of ten people said they would consider coming to

church if someone they knew invited them, but they would not come if a stranger invited them.

- They remind the child that the children's club is on. Children often resemble goldfish in the memory department.
- They remind the parent that the children's club is on. Parents often resemble their children who resemble the goldfish in the memory department.
- From time to time they allow you the opportunity to invite the parents to wider church activities, for example, Alpha, Easter services and Christmas carol services.

Because of the work we do before we open clubs we usually start with a fairly large number. We have visited the school, we have sent a mail-shot to all our contacts, we have advertised where possible and we may even have given an incentive for children to come, for example a free chocolate bar. However, from then on we often just accept the number of children who come, forgetting all the work that was necessary for high attendance in the first place!

Therefore, tackle the situation on two levels.

- We visit each child who attends. We do this every week.
- We repeat every week the processes that gave us the high attendance for the first week: we advertise, we may offer an incentive, we visit the school.

 WARNING: Have clear rules for home visits. You may wish to adopt the following:

- Workers must NEVER:
- Enter the home if only a child is there
- Enter the home if only the parent of the opposite sex is there.
- Workers must take proper precautions if they intend to visit after dark. If you have to visit after dark:
- Ensure somebody knows where you are
- Inform them when you start
- Inform them when you finish.

Children who live further away from the church should be sent the colouring competition by email. It is of course probable that you could contact all the children by email. But don't be tempted to short cut the development of relationship that visiting gives. If it really is impossible, then email three weeks out of four, and visit on the fourth.

By the time the child attends for Week 2, their name should be on the register. At the end of the academic year spend some time cleaning up your database. Make sure the youth department has been given the names and addresses of the children eligible to move up. Delete the names of children who've moved out of the area. Delete the names of children who you know will no longer be attending for whatever reason.

Community events

Whether we choose to plant "stand alone" children's clubs or whether we start our children's club in the church itself, reaching parents is still an important part of the process. I've listed some ideas that will enable you to do this. The list is not exhaustive, it's intended to give some ideas that you can develop, so use your imagination.

PARENTS' MEAL WITH CHILDREN'S TALENT SHOW

Produce nice invitations and ask the children to invite their parents, their grannies and whoever else they know. Entrance should be by ticket only and the price of the ticket should cover your costs – unless it is a fundraiser as well, in which case it should have the profit margin you are looking for added to it.

Children are always keen to show off and this gives them the perfect opportunity. Make it a candlelit meal, ask the children to dress in black trousers/skirts and white shirt if they are serving. Escort the parents to their table, play background music, go for it! After dessert and coffee the children will then perform. This is a fabulous way to introduce parents to your building. And to make it more effective make sure your tables contain a mixture of people who already come to your church and people who don't.

A note of warning. Make sure you've seen the talent show items before the talent show. Many a good children's worker has come unstuck because they haven't known what is coming up!

FAMILY FUN DAY

From 10 a.m. until 2 p.m. Bouncy castles are always the key to making life easy, but construct the day as if it were a fairground. Coconut shies, leaders in stocks, throw the ball through the hole, penalty shoot-out area. A soft play area for toddlers, face painters, maybe a children's entertainer on hand. A barbecue is essential, maybe even some candy-floss. Invites freely available to forthcoming church services. Visit a fairground and let your imagination run riot.

BARN DANCE

This still works. Parents will come out to a barn dance and because of the nature of barn dancing, everyone gets to meet everyone else. It is a splendid way for people to meet others. However, it is worth getting a general feel for prospective attendance beforehand. An empty barn dance is rarely a successful event.

BARBECUE AND ENTERTAINER

The end of the summer term is an excellent time for this particular activity. Invite all the parents to the end-of-term family barbecue. The first forty-five minutes will be taken up by a children's entertainer who will do clowning, illusions and general entertainment for the children. The barbecue will take place in the second forty-five minutes. Persuade the entertainer to stay until the end. He can wander freely among the crowd doing balloon modelling, plate spinning, and so on. Hire a bouncy castle. Play background music.

SPECIALS

If you are able to get special performers to come to your venue these are prime times to ensure you have invited all the parents and the wider community. The African Children's Choir recently did a tour of the UK and were looking for venues to perform in – check out their website and look to book them in the future as they will pack any event they perform in. If you can't get the African Children's Choir then maybe organize your own "All Nations Event" and invite those from various ethnic backgrounds to come and perform.

SPORTS EVENING

Hold a sports evening for the children and invite the parents to come and watch. Hold the usual parents' races and give out prizes. The only caution here is to ensure that some of the parents don't get over-competitive; some parents have come to blows over the outcome of the egg and spoon race!

WARNING: All of these events work most effectively in the context of established relationships. Parents who have been visited on a regular basis are more likely to attend events; people with whom you have developed a relationship are more likely to attend your church services if you invite them. It's all about forming honest, real and authentic relationships.

HIRE A LOCAL SWIMMING POOL

Hire the local swimming pool for the evening and invite all the parents of the children who attend your activities. Make a special note with this one that children are not allowed to come alone; they must come with a parent or guardian. If children come by themselves you may have all sorts of problems with child to adult ratios in the water. At the end of the night maybe provide hot chocolate and chips back at the church.

PANTOMIME OR MUSICAL

If you have the time and the talent then maybe put together a musical or pantomime for the wider community to come and view. Several years ago we presented *Joseph and the Amazing Technicolor Dreamcoat* and over 500 people from our community came to see the production. As an extension to this idea, invite members of the community to become part of the production as actors, technical people, costume makers, caterers. The sense of friendship developed in producing live performances can easily be translated to attendance in church. Once again relationship is the key.

CHRISTINGLE

This event cannot be omitted. It is a wonderful way of drawing in huge numbers of families. Christingle is a custom which originated in the Moravian Church in 1747. It involves children making a Christingle using an orange, some sweets, a candle, some ribbon and a few cocktail sticks. For comprehensive information you will need to go to The Children's Society web page (www.childrenssociety.org.uk/what-you-can-do/fundraising-and-events/christingle-resources) and look at the detailed instructions, including a template for the order of service. The service usually takes place on Christmas Eve at approximately 4 or 5 p.m. and lasts for one hour. It is perfect for parents who want to do something with their children before Christmas Eve dinner and early bedtime! If publicized well this service should result in a packed church with a further opportunity to advertise all your Christmas and New Year services. The advertising could take the form of a leaflet to the local primary schools that explain the significance of the Christingle and provide instructions of how to make them. The children could even bring their own Christingle with them on the evening.

OPEN NIGHT

Parents are often curious about what goes on at the children's club. Hold an open night where parents can come and stand at the back and watch what goes on. Maybe involve them in some of the games. Don't water down your presentation for this evening, for two reasons:
- It is right and proper that parents get to see exactly what you teach their children.
- Your presentation to children may win some parents to Jesus; it will not be the first time this has happened.

> COMMENT: You would think that events that are free would attract more people than those that cost something. Amazingly this does not seem to be the case. I suspect in some parents' minds events that cost nothing are worth nothing. They would prefer to feel that they are supporting something. So "Come to the talent show, cost is £1 per person with all profits going to the children's club" will give you a higher attendance than "Come to the talent show – it's free". Strange, but absolutely true!

End every event with something like the following:

> It has been great to see you all here this evening and I trust you enjoyed yourselves. Just to let you know that [MY CHURCH] is primarily a church. It exists to let people know that God loves them. We have a church meeting here tomorrow at 11 a.m. and every Sunday at the same time; you are very welcome to attend. Again, thank you for coming and we hope to see you very soon.

Try to have a flyer advertising your next event for people to take away with them. On the back should be a list of your regular church activities and a contact number for enquiries. **You will be surprised how many calls you receive from people who only ever came to one of your events but when they hit crisis it's your church they call**.

Do not preach on these occasions unless it becomes very natural to do so. Do not make appeals. Do not become fanatical. These are just awareness events. They are designed for people to see you in a non-threatening atmosphere and for them to begin to understand that Christians can be fairly normal too – well most of them!

FIRST CONTACT (SCHOOLS MINISTRY)

When I was writing the first incarnation of this book my daughter had just started school. It was an emotional morning. She was very excited. My wife and I were very nervous. She put on her little school uniform. She collected her packed lunch with the obligatory Barbie logo. She put on her newly polished shoes and took her mother's hand for the short journey to school. She loved it. She talked about it all evening. Then, just after her bedtime story, she looked serious and said, "Daddy, do I have to go to school for a long time?"

She was four at the time. Now, she has just left for university. The uniform is different and the logos are very different, but my wife and I were still nervous. She has already spent fourteen years in the education system. She took a year out last year to work with Edge Church Adelaide, but now she is back in education for at least another three years. At least seventeen years in the education system. This is the reality. Thousands and thousands of children every day make their way to school. If we want to talk to children, then that's where they are. And while I know that opportunities to have input to schools varies all over the world, there is usually a way for the creatives.

In the UK, as well as the countless number of church schools, there exists at present an opening for followers of Jesus to have input into a huge number of non-church schools – as governors, as Christian teachers, but also as children and family workers who visit schools for the purpose of taking Christian assemblies or religious education classes.

Being able to work in schools is a major opportunity. Taking school assemblies means that you can stand in front of hundreds of children, who are supervised by school teachers, and within certain limits share the principles of God's word. If you are good at what you do and the school staff warm to you then you could be invited in at ever-increasing frequency. The law requires that schools provide Christian assemblies, but teachers for the most part don't like taking assemblies (when I talked to a teacher about this she mentioned standing in front of the children is not the thing that puts them off, it is the number of other teachers watching. Clearly teachers who are not Christians themselves sometimes find it difficult to present Christian assemblies). Schools will be very keen to have your input, but herein lies the problem: you could get to the point where the school would like you to come in several times a week. A huge percentage of your time could be spent in schools. Before this happens it is important to know why you are there.

Over recent years schools ministry has gained an increasingly greater profile, and a very large number of churches now have input into local schools. However it is not legitimate to have input into schools just because everyone else is doing it! There are two legitimate reasons to be involved in schools ministry:

1. To be salt and light

The Bible is clear that the Kingdom of God is within us. When a Christian enters a school the Kingdom of God comes to the school. Simply because a Christian is there the light begins to shine. Before we say a word, the light begins to shine. Going into schools to bring salt and light is a worthwhile investment. Hundreds of children will be able to see and hear Jesus in you. **We may be the only Christians some of these children ever see and we should never undervalue our role or our responsibility**.

2. As a means of drawing children into your children's club

Children who see you in school assembly may want to come to your children's club because you've personally invited them. Parents may be more inclined to allow their children to come to your children's club because they know that you are allowed into their school.

WARNING: Because of the above I recommend that you do not advertise your children's club in a school unless you have had input into that school for at least six months. It will take you six months to build a relationship with the school and the head teacher. Relationship is everything. With the best intent in the world sometimes things go wrong at children's clubs. A broken bone on a bouncy castle, a child who runs off early and takes hours to be found, a fight... the list is endless. If something goes wrong in your club and you have only been in the school for a few weeks the negative effect may cause problems in the club and the school may close the door to you. If, however, you have a working relationship then most head teachers will allow you to explain the difficulty and since most experienced heads have encountered every difficulty known to man, with the possible exception of plague and famine, they will understand that sometimes things go wrong.

Many churches have built strong and well-attended children's clubs by focusing on schools ministry. Even children's workers who are not full time may be able to find the several hours a week (or possibly a month) that it takes to give input into the school. "Open the Book" works on the basis of a small team going into a school once a week to read a story from Bob Hartman's *The Lion Storyteller Bible*. It can be a very simple reading, or the group can act parts out, or use props they have made or get the children involved – all dependent on the ability and skills of the team. They then go to someone's house nearby for a coffee and to sort out the following week. There is no searching for ideas, no pressure, and it is being undertaken by young mums and retired people, who may have not got involved otherwise.

The best scenario is a combination of (1) and (2). Be salt and light, but also use the opportunity to populate your children's programmes.

So you've worked out why you want to have input, but now how do you get into the school?

The importance of prayer should never be overlooked. Your presence in school is of vital significance. Light is about to enter a place and any lurking darkness will not be too pleased. Therefore, before you attempt to make contact, pray. Make it a theme for your prayer meetings; ask people to make it part of their daily devotions.

COMMENT: It is unfortunate that over the many years I have been involved in schools I have always had less of a problem gaining access and consistently inputting into the school when the head teacher has been an agnostic or atheist than when the head teacher has been of a religious persuasion. I have always done my utmost not to fly denominational colours when entering a school, but when the head teacher is a Baptist he wants Baptist input. When the head teacher is from a Pentecostal background she wants Pentecostal input. This is complete nonsense. We need as much CHRISTIAN input into a school as possible and fighting our party's position is at best very counterproductive.

Once you have prayed and made the whole thing a matter of ongoing prayer it is useful to enquire whether there is a Christian teacher in the school that might invite you in, or recommend you to the person who does the inviting. If there is nobody in the school who can recommend you then phone the school and ask for ten minutes with the head teacher to discuss your request. In my last church, being true to my word, schools work was the first thing I did. I arrived at one of our schools within a week of moving in and told the receptionist who I was and asked if the head had a spare ten minutes. The receptionist scurried off and then came back and escorted me to the head teacher's office. I explained that I was new, but I loved taking school assemblies and if she would let me come and talk to her children, I would love it. More importantly I promised that the children would love it too. She invited me in the following morning and I was a regular visitor for the next seven years. I did the same with all the schools in my area. It's not hard. I have now taken over 3,000 school assemblies and I still love the feeling of talking to children in a school assembly. I like it even more when parents are allowed in to listen, at Christmas or Easter or harvest, or at least one of our schools, every Friday!

Without doubt it is the first school you ever make contact with that is the hardest. I have now taken so many school assemblies I don't have a problem with them any more. If I have to change areas or want to make contact with new schools then I ask the old schools for a reference – although it has been so easy to gain entrance in the last decade or so I have rarely had to use them.

> TIP: If you have a church building, whether modern or traditional, schools may like to visit it as part of the national curriculum. This is a great way of meeting teachers and forming relationships. Drop a letter into the schools near you and mention that you are willing for schools to visit. Say that you would be happy to give a tour and explain what happens on Sundays, etc.

First contact

When you are scheduled to be in school you should always be professional, be courteous and helpful, particularly to the secretary you meet at reception – a primary school secretary carries a lot more responsibility and influence than we would ever warrant. They can be the gatekeeper – don't upset them! Arrive on time, calm and relaxed – this will put all those around you into a similar frame of mind. Now balance all that with the fact that you are the ambassador of the King of all kings and life comes to every place where you step. It's a tricky balance – to walk with boldness and humility.

CONDUCTING THE ASSEMBLY OR LESSON

You may be asked how you want to be introduced. I always opt for the simplest response, "Tell them my name is Mark and I've come to talk to them." No denominational ties, no titles, no frills, just me. This generation doesn't understand denominations and the generation before them has very little respect for authority.

Be fun, be entertaining, but don't be the clown. Conduct the assembly with the same standards of discipline as the head teacher would. When you stand at the front then you are in charge. Don't be afraid to ask a child who is misbehaving to stop.

What do you talk about?

Here are some pointers.

- Be relevant, talk about bullies, heroes, worries, caring and divorce.
- Use stories, drama, object lessons and involvement.
- Don't just give the children information, teach them how to learn.

And I would also suggest having a copy of my *Hanging on Every Word* at hand for the times when you need some help at very short notice! Schools are not always predictable.

Staying in

So you are in. How do you stay in? As in most areas of Christian ministry, relationship is the key. It may seem like a waste of time to sit in a staffroom drinking coffee, but this is the place where the teachers are making decisions on whether they would like you back or not. Be friendly, be approachable, be fun. Here are some basics:

- learn the head teacher's name
- show authentic interest in the school
- always send Christmas cards
- be human!
- never carry gossip about one school to another
- never let the school down unless you are dying or dead!

> COMMENT: Organize an Easter and a Christmas "learning event" at your church and invite Year 6 children from your local schools to come to it. It should run for no more than ninety minutes and those schools that are within walking distance should be invited. Start with an introductory ice breaker, then an open talk time, a worksheet time, and conclude with a time for the children to make something themselves. Talk about the true origins of Christmas (don't criticize Santa – this will prove very counterproductive and you may be crossed off his Christmas Eve visiting list!). Talk about the significance of Easter for Christians, show the objects used in Communion. You will find a good take up from schools for this type of event.

Administration – making life simpler

I send out a letter every term (a sample is shown in Appendix 1). In early September I will send out a letter advertising the assemblies available for October, November and December. The schools will then phone or email and book an assembly date for September, October, November and December. By mid-September all my administration regarding schools is complete and I can concentrate on taking assemblies. It really is quite liberating. I then send out a letter in December for January, February and March and a final letter in April for June and July. I don't take assemblies in April because of the huge amount of school holidays there and I don't take assemblies in May because that's my month for refocusing. If I can book school visits for the next three months before leaving the school, so much the better. I then promise to send on a letter confirming themes.

Once I have developed an assembly and used it for the whole month I write it up properly and place it in a file with all the necessary visuals. I now have forty-five key assemblies that I rotate on a five-year cycle. Or did have. I get bored easily, so I like to drop new ones in and old ones out. Check out *The Day the Crayons Quit* by Drew Daywalt, it's my most recent find for a school story.

I also tend to offer assemblies in threes that follow this pattern:

- Month 1: Moral teaching that may have a limited Christian content
- Month 2: Much stronger Christian content

- Month 3: Strong Christian content (Christmas and Easter usually fall in my third month).

The Day the Crayons Quit would be a typical Month 1 story.

> WARNING: It is possible to be too popular! When I was in Milton Keynes I quickly arrived at the point where most of the sixty-six primary schools within the city welcomed my input. It is tempting to visit them all. But can we really outwork our purposes in every school? It is best to mark yourself a geographical limit – I will visit schools within three miles of the church only – or I will only visit schools within my parish boundary. I may visit other schools but only for specials: harvest festivals, Christmas, Easter, OFSTED inspection.
> In reality I have always found it very hard to say no and still sometimes travel 8 or 9 km to take an assembly – you don't have to follow my bad habits!

But before we leave this section allow me to emphasize again how vital this area is. And how much of an opportunity it can be. It really is the golden bullet for countries that still allow input into schools. If every church in the country gave regular input into their local schools then it would mean that every child in the country hears the good news of Jesus on an ongoing basis. It really is a gift, please don't overlook it.

Social media

It is undoubtedly important at this point to mention social media. Whatever we may feel about our Facebook/Instagram/Twitter/Snapchat, etc., obsessed culture, there is no point denying that they can be useful tools. So open a Facebook page with your event names. There is no problem if you end up with three of them, you can always encourage people to "like" other pages once they join one, and get parents on the page ASAP. Now you have quick points of contact. Remember this is Facebook; their policy doesn't allow under thirteens on there, and also keep all your conversations in public if at all possible. Add an Instagram account and push your photos out, and then a Twitter account in case you're missing anyone, and then join them altogether. So you post on one and it appears on all the rest. If this is all beyond you, then you'll need to find yourself a consultant to help you. I would suggest that seven-year-olds make the best consultants!

Once you are up and running, keep the pages populated. When I look at a Facebook page and see no activity for the last six months, I conclude the club has closed. Keep it working. Add videos, adverts, interviews, upcoming events. And of course you join it altogether and advertise one activity on the other activity page and you're away.

The rule of thumb is this: if you can, visit. If you can't visit, schools work and social media can keep you going. If you can do all three, you'll consistently see growth...

BREAKING NEW GROUND

I recently stood in a theological college that trains ministers and asked them the following question:

> If 80 per cent of our churchgoers become Christians before they are eighteen then why do we concentrate most of our evangelism on those outside this age group? And why don't we rethink the whole thing and plant some children's churches that will grow into youth churches that will grow into fully formed family churches?

After the look of abject horror, some answers began to emerge:
- existing leaders will not accept it
- it's not financially viable
- it's never been done like that
- it won't work
- it's not biblical
- it undermines the concept of family.

Interestingly enough some of these same objections were thrown at Jesus. Some of them need to be dumped instantly. What other people think of us should never colour what we do. Paul said, "It has always been my ambition to preach the gospel where Christ was not known, so that I would not be building on someone else's foundation" (Romans 15:20, NIV).

So is it possible? There are now some very significant churches around that started life as children's clubs. Clearly, it has been done. The programme outlined in the "Beginner's Guide" section on page 217 is designed to show you how to start a children's club within your church. However, it has been constructed in such a way as to make it "freestanding" for those God calls in this direction. By "freestanding" I don't mean without covering or affiliation. Churches can be built from children's clubs, but these children's clubs must have a line of accountability and covering that runs back to a local church that can provide input, advice, teaching and training, and when everyone gets a little older... babysitters! I am not actually a fan of single-generational models of church, but if we are using them as a way of planting new churches that will eventually become intergenerational, then there must certainly be a place for them.

Paul is one of our best examples of an apostle, and he gives us an insight into the apostolic heart when he writes, that he longs to plant on virgin soil. There are countless housing estates, city centre blocks of flats and other urban developments that will not be reached by a normal church plant. The parents in these places may never respond. Does this mean we ignore the children? We have an opportunity to change life patterns, to grab hold of a downward spiral and bring the gospel of Christ to others. Will these parents allow their children to attend a children's club? Yes! For some reason there is still a positive residual effect. Parents believe that these clubs will do their children good. I happen to agree with them. Let's consider planting some.

Singing and prayer

The components that make up a great children's, youth or family ministry have been relatively unchanged for centuries. By the late eighteenth century the pattern was fixed, although we have continued to play with the terminology:

- prayer/talking to Jesus
- singing/worship
- teaching/sermon/talk.

In more recent centuries we have woven a range of activities into the pattern – whether it be the activity sessions and shared meal/snack of Lucy Moore's extraordinary Messy Church programme (explored more fully later, p. 118) or the free play model outlined in my children's outreach club pattern (p. 220). And of course youth and children's programmes have been weaving in games and ice breakers and testimonies for quite some time; the more charismatic of us have added response and ministry times at the end and extended the singing/worship slot.

But I would suggest these are important foundation stones of any evangelistic programme. If any of these elements are missing there will always be the risk of developing a social activity rather than an evangelistic activity. Time has already been given to the teaching/sermon/talk part of this when we touched on communication in an earlier chapter, but allow me to make a few observations on prayer and singing.

Prayer

Prayer is talking to God. But more than that it is connecting with Him. Most evangelistic projects have prayer involved somewhere, but it can quickly be observed that prayer falls into a very narrow band of categories:

- Children/families prayed for by the leader at the start of the event.
- Children/families repeating a prayer that the leader prays.
- Children/families prayed for by various team members.

But what is often lacking is space that allows children/families to pray themselves. Space given for children and parents to talk to God personally. Space given to allow connection. Space given that allows encounter to occur. It is significantly important. The concern is that people attend our events and have a vicarious relationship with Jesus. They live their Christian life through us rather than having a personal relationship themselves. Discipleship means teaching them to connect with Jesus themselves.

Singing

It is interesting to watch the different emphasis on singing through the centuries. Today we talk about worship and the need for intimacy in our singing. But at the start of this glorious thing called child evangelism, singing was for a very different purpose – primarily to teach theology through song. What we must be careful of is confusing style for depth.

But at the same time, our songs, whether they are designed to allow us to draw close to God or not, really should teach us theology. Allow me a few examples. This hymn from the fifteenth century, translated in the eighteenth century, would have been sung in the early Sunday schools:

> Praise to the Lord, the Almighty, the King of creation!
> O my soul, praise him, for he is thy health and salvation!
> All ye who hear,
> now to his temple draw near;
> praise him in glad adoration.

It's a song about creation. But putting the melody to one side, so is this more recent song, used by permission of my friend Doug Horley:

> He made dogs that point, pigs that oink,
> he made dolphin smiles, crocodiles,
> He made a zillion things, flies and wings.
> He even gave us tongues so good for licking.
> And it's lovely jubbly, all of God's creation.
> Lovely jubbly, all of God's creation,
> what a wonderful God we have.[25]

And I know there are newer examples, even from Doug himself, but I like this one. And hymns such as:

> Fight the good fight with all thy might,
> Christ is thy strength and Christ thy right;
> lay hold on life, and it shall be
> thy joy and crown eternally.

When given the Doug Horley treatment become:

> I'm gonna jump up and down,
> gonna spin right around, gonna praise your
> Name forever, gonna shout out loud,
> gonna deafen the crowd
> gonna send my praise to heaven

---

25   Doug Horley, "Lovely Jubbly", Thankyou Music, 2001.

I'll follow Jesus 'til the day I DROP.
I can do all things through,
Christ who strengthens me

When you've got such a lot,

When you've got not a lot.

What? Be happy![26]

Two hymns that appear very different on first examination, but at their core they both speak of persevering in the Christian faith. The style has changed radically; the theological sentiment has not.

There is one more observation to be made in this section and it relates to a slightly scary word called "sacramental". It needs drawing attention to because in the most recent surveys children complained![27] They said they loved their children's club, but when it came to the prayer, singing, teaching time they wanted to do more. It was pointed out that they get to do lots of actions in the songs, but apparently that wasn't enough. When further questions were asked it transpired that they wanted to make sacramental responses to their prayers and to the teaching. Sacramental with a small "s". They wanted to do something externally to show something that was happening internally. They wanted to light candles, they wanted to pour water, they wanted to be able to sit and write their own prayers. They wanted to do more. It's definitely worth experimenting.

Rewards and prizes

Before we leave the eighteenth century, there are examples of incentives being given for children to attend the outreach children's clubs. Raikes himself gave bookmarks and combs (I'm not sure combs would work any more) as an incentive for boys and girls to attend the prayer meetings at Gloucester Cathedral at 7 on Sunday mornings. Here's a wonderful quote from Robert Raikes, spoken in 1783: "These little ragamuffins have taken it into their heads to frequent the early

---

26   Doug Horley, "Be Happy", Thankyou Music, 2001.
27   Codrington, G. T., unpublished Masters thesis, 1999.

morning prayers which are held at the Cathedral at seven o' clock. I believe there were nearly fifty there this morning."[28]

There are often concerns raised about the giving of prizes but the practice is widespread. Several of the schools I have visited gave "Star of the Week" certificates out or put children's names in the "Golden Book" and read out those names in school assemblies. But I would be quick to add an important caveat to this area, which in fairness the schools do well with their Golden Book policy: don't just reward sporting achievement, that is, the child who runs the fastest, balances the best, and so on. And don't just reward intelligence. Whatever that word actually means, it is usually attributed to those who know the answers to all the questions. Also, reward character. Reward kindness and compassion. The child that holds the door open as you stumble through it with arms full of equipment. Reward the boy or girl who sits with the new child who is feeling a little upset, arm around them bringing comfort.

In terms of the children's outreach club, nobody uses prizes and incentives as well as Bill Wilson of the aforementioned Metro World Child. Hundreds of children gather in front of him and as he approaches preaching time, balloons can be seen behind him, three for each team. The instructions are given out.

> We're moving into preaching time. Everybody needs to sit with their hands in their lap. If you are completely silent and really listening, then a leader may put a prize in your hands. At the end of today, everyone is going to get a prize. Unless you talk or mess around. If you talk, one of your balloons will be burst. If all three of your balloons are burst then your team will not get any prizes, and all your prizes will go to the other team.[29]

It seems a little heavy, but remember the instructions on what we need to recruit when we are employing children's workers:

- someone who can communicate Jesus
- someone who can keep control.

---

28   Robert Raikes to Richard Townley, published by Townley in the *Manchester Mercury*, 6 January 1784, quoted in my *One Generation from Extinction*, Oxford: Monarch, 2009.
29   Bill Wilson, Metro World Child.

If there is no control structure, then nobody is listening and the message is lost. Our message is too important to lose.

The challenge of smaller groups

There are often objections listed to running this sort of children's project. But the most common I hear runs like this:

> This is all well and good but we have twenty children at our club and our entire village only has thirty children; how can we outwork what we have just read?

> My wife is sixty-five and I'm seventy. We run a children's club for a dozen children each week; some of the things mentioned in this book seem unattainable to us.

But I am a strong advocate that there will always be children who need to hear about Jesus. And you never quite know who will be in your group, small though it may be. Let me demonstrate:

> In a small church in Scotland in the 1800s the elders of a church gathered for a special meeting. The subject under consideration was the future of their minister. He was getting quite old and the only work of any significance he had undertaken in the last year was to run a Sunday school in which a nine-year-old boy had made the decision to serve Jesus. It didn't take the elders long to reach their decision. The minister was asked to step down.
>
> They did not understand the significance of that little Sunday school and the impact that little boy would have. Don't be discouraged by your small group. **Be encouraged that you are doing what God has called you to do and although you may never see it, the impact of your ministry will have eternal significance. You will touch the future.**
>
> The little boy grew up. His name was Robert Moffat. He is considered to be the founder of modern missions. In one address in an English university he said this, "There is a land in the north of Africa that has never been reached with the gospel. I saw the smoke of a thousand villages that have never heard the gospel. Who will go?"

A young man in the audience answered in his heart "I will go." And he did. His name was David Livingstone. Africa owes much to that Scottish minister who did nothing of apparent significance that year – only leading a nine-year-old child to Christ!

There are surprisingly very few differences between talking to a small group and a large group. Let me try and identify the main features that need addressing:

The incentive system for reinforcing positive behaviour

I find larger groups much easier to control. In the most simplistic sense, by splitting the large group into three teams with a system in place to reinforce positive behaviour and to deter negative behaviour, the groups naturally form into three individual and distinct groups. The groups control themselves. A child who is talking in a quiet time will be told in no uncertain terms by the rest of the group to stop before he gives points to the other teams. In a small group the individuals remain as individuals and the incentive must be more personal.

WARNING: Children under seven have very little understanding of gaining and losing points for their team. They will sit like angels if they feel they will get a personal benefit, but they are not particularly interested in the team. They learn this concept a little later in their social development, but it is worth knowing so that a little grace can be shown to this age group.

For a smaller group consider constructing a star chart (or a more creative alternative). The children should get a star for attendance, another for good behaviour, another for doing their best, another for memorizing Bible texts. A small prize may be given at the end of each session or the stars may mount up the whole term and the winner gets a large prize. You may be concerned that this becomes a little competitive. Maybe give a prize to everyone who has five stars or more but give one big prize to the overall winner – this way everyone wins.

The degree of interaction changes

To communicate well to a smaller group will involve talking to individuals and getting feedback. Involvement is a key to communication in groups of all sizes, but it is incredibly important with smaller groups. Keep them involved by asking them questions, asking them to hold objects for object lessons, involve them as characters in stories, and keep keeping them involved.

The relationship dynamic changes

Consider the points we made earlier. If:

- they do not like you they will not listen to you
- you will not listen to them they will not listen to you
- you will not have fun with them they will not listen to you.

Now multiply these factors by 100 and you begin to understand smaller group relationship dynamics.

With smaller groups the need for regular outings and fun times increases greatly. You have the opportunity for much greater input in their lives, you have the opportunity to show them Jesus in you as well as telling them about the Jesus in you.

Some of the most fruitful children's workers only work with small groups. They understand the significance of pouring themselves into a few. Interestingly and rather obviously Jesus chose to work with small groups.

Ever heard of Edward Kimball? I hadn't until recently. But this man is a hero who was at the head of a dazzling line of ministers. Edward Kimball worked with children and in 1858 he led a young boy named Dwight to Jesus. Dwight grew up to be known as D. L. Moody. In turn, Moody led a young man named F. B. Meyer to Jesus; F. B. Meyer was to lead J. W. Chapman to Jesus; Chapman led Billy Sunday to Jesus; Billy Sunday led Mordecai Ham to Jesus, and Ham, in turn, led Billy Graham to Jesus. So don't worry about numbers; win children to Jesus.

A Case Study: Messy Church in Practice — Rachel Hill-Brown

While it would be of some use to outline the characteristics of Messy Church, Lucy Moore has already done this and numerous books are available for those who would like to know more. What I hope will be far more useful is to show the history of development of an actual Messy Church project with all the associated ministries that have grown out of it. Below therefore is the account of the Messy Church established and developed by Revd Rachel Hill-Brown. It highlights well the joy of Messy Church in that while the discussion groups are still trying to understand how it can be used to make disciples and discussing matters of ecclesiology, Messy Church itself has burst its banks and all sorts of wonderful initiatives are developing around it.

We started Messy Church in January 2013. Prior to this our parish had, for over ten years, run a very successful annual children's holiday club which had hundreds of children attending. It took place in our church school during the summer holidays. However, it was increasingly clear that this annual event was not having an ongoing impact for children and families and that relationships established were not given the chance to grow. Very few children and families joined the regular worshipping community. This does not undermine the quality of the holiday clubs or the fun that the children had or the seeds of faith that were planted. But it was felt that the time had come to do something different. Something that meant relationships had a chance to grow and Messy Church seemed to be a creative, regular way to do this while also providing the opportunity to pass on the faith from generation to generation – in whole families, not just to children.

We worked hard to research the best time to hold our Messy Church and spent time exploring the values of Messy Church together among the team that expressed interest in helping set it up. Most of them still continue to resource it. We decided, after talking to some local families about what a good time would be, to meet on a Sunday afternoon in the school hall (which is also a designated worship space) at 3.30 p.m. This seemed to be a good time for our local community because football and clubs were finished for the weekend and 3.30 p.m. was something of an empty space. Meeting at this time provides the opportunity for whole families, including dads and often grandparents too, to attend and join in together.

We quickly established a regular monthly attendance of over 100 and average around 150. This is both fantastic and a challenge. It is fantastic because we are clearly doing something that people enjoy and come back to. We have been determined to provide good quality in all we do. Good coffee, good biscuits, Sunday papers, a safe crèche area, coat racks, good food – and plenty of it!

It is a challenge because of the scale of the resourcing it requires. It is a bit of a military operation to set up, feed and provide activities for that number of people. It is also difficult to find ways of helping people to "own" Messy Church. But we have got some families who now help with clearing up, washing-up and cake making.

In three and a half years we have over 400 people who have attended Messy Church and a core group of regular attenders (those who come more than half the time) who number just over 200. We have a core group planning team which meets every two months to plan, review and pray. We also look at ways to improve what we do, so recently we started a "prayer tent" gazebo that we locate in different places each month and use to encourage families to actively engage with prayer. We cater for a range of dietary requirements and have a number of children with additional needs who attend. It has become a safe place for a number of families who struggle with the structure and perceived expectations of more traditional services.

It quickly became evident that such large numbers meant that the aim of developing relationships was challenged by what sometimes felt like "industrial scale" Messy Church. Investing in relationships is key to growing communities of faith and allowing space for individuals to ask questions, seek support and explore life together is hugely important. So this need to provide further opportunities to engage with children and families has meant that we have gradually developed a range of other groups and opportunities. We had also learned that the core values of Messy Church – being intergenerational, hospitality, creativity and being Christ-centred – are key and effective. That has inspired us to develop new ways of "being" based on these values.

We have had over a dozen baptisms from Messy church – of adults, children and babies. This has included baptisms at Messy Church itself as well as at other times and in other services.

Year 5/6 cell group

First we started a midweek cell group for children aged nine to eleven. This was quite strategic in that research shows clearly that children of this age are making serious decisions about life and where they belong as well as matters of faith. They have a strong need for belonging and being part of a group and also have a strong sense of justice and a desire to explore life and world issues. While our church had a thriving Sunday school on a Sunday morning, a significant number of families were not attending at that time so were "missing out". Hence setting up the group in September 2013. Each year this group has grown as the children have brought friends along. Their commitment to the group has been impressive with children attending very regularly and showing a high level of commitment to the group and each other. Each session involves games, eating pizza and some teaching input about engaging actively with faith. The group is around twelve strong and now called PJs – Pizza and Jesus! Our sessions are timed so that the midweek Youth Club starts soon after we finish and that means there is opportunity for the children to be aware of what they have to look forward to and to begin to get to know the youth team. At least once each term the Youth Worker joins us at PJs. These young people show a high level of commitment to everything they do. They love to bless other groups who are part of the wider worshipping community.

Messy Café

Messy Café started in December 2015 and meets monthly on a Friday morning in the school hall after collective worship and before nursery pick up. It is aimed at anyone and everyone and is a drop-in café which also has activities for pre-school children to engage with as well. This has been a place where significant conversations have taken place, including baptism requests. It has provided a space to meet up with people strategically as well as incidentally. A number of initial baptism enquiries have been expressed during café. It is a smaller (forty to fifty people) group allowing for more relaxed and in-depth conversations and connections to be made. It is another intergenerational opportunity that helps link people together, provide support, and gives the opportunity to invite folk to other things that are going on.

Monday mums

This group started in January 2016. This is a daytime group of mums who attend Messy Church and some other services that we provide. None of them were in a home group before and they come from a range of places in terms of faith. We meet weekly, with some of our younger children playing at our feet, and have started by using Nooma DVDs to talk about life and faith together and to begin to pray for one another. This group of twelve mums come when they can and are all at the stage of life where their children and working patterns are in a constant state of flux. The relationships have grown and deepened and so has confidence in prayer. More recently members are beginning to invite friends to come along too. So, natural, organic growth is occurring. This group has attracted new members as some have had to stop coming for other commitments. It is relaxed group that meets with the smallest children at their feet as they explore living a life of faith with each other.

Club JC

Club JC is our Sunday school which meets during the Sunday morning service. This is a group of up to forty children of families who attend this service. Until Easter 2016 it took the form of traditional Sunday school with children going off to smaller spaces and age-related groups. However, there were a number of children who were not enjoying this "school-based approach" and we had learned from Messy Church that children of all ages enjoy being together, learning and playing together. Added to this was the challenge of a building that was less than ideal. We have children with additional needs who need access to both kitchen and toilet facilities, so from Easter 2016 we moved to a new way of doing Club JC in which all three to elevens go into the hall together. We have a crèche area on the edge of the space too so the under threes are also part of what we are doing together. We now also follow the same readings and themes that the main congregation do in the service. We start all together with some teaching input and worship before moving to a range of self-selected activities relating to the theme. We are able to work with particular groups on particular activities as well as allowing free play and whole group games. The children are happy, engaged, becoming friends across the age range and have a much stronger sense of belonging. We are also able to include the children with additional needs more easily and safely. We recently had a Light Party which was facilitated by an external group and gave an extended time for the children to participate in worship as well to engage with and respond to Christian teaching. Sixty children aged five to eleven attended and they were almost all part of the worshipping community – children who are part of the wider life of the church and its activities. We hope these will become a regular (twice yearly) feature of what we do.

Breakfast Church

Breakfast Church started in September 2016. It is clearly and intentionally all-age and is based on hospitality as we eat breakfast together. It is timed to finish in time for Sunday morning activities (8.45 a.m. to 9.45 a.m.) and provides opportunities to engage with creative and interactive activities and to pray in different ways together. This includes making something and a table talk card which relates to the theme that is on the table to encourage conversation. We include sung worship, teaching and prayer. We also include testimony and a quiz. We provide a safe space for younger children, high chairs and food which takes account of dietary requirements. We have already seen this engage with a significant number of "Messy Church" families and some whom we have never seen at other services too. It is effective as an all-age service because it focuses on hospitality rather than wanting to try and fit in something for everyone. Children remain engaged and people talk together across age groups. This service is enabling whole families to come to church together as well as supporting them in their wider family life. We have 120 people coming with around forty-five children. A more traditional service follows Breakfast Church with coffee continuing between the services. We still see some families with children attending this service.

Since January 2016 the diocese has partly funded a Children's and Families' Missioner for the parish. With significant work going on with children and families before this appointment it has meant that continuing growth has happened naturally and organically but with the resourcing and leadership to enable it to do so. The PCC has set aside a generous budget for work with children and families which means we can provide good quality in what we do. We don't charge for anything, but we do ask for donations and encourage those who would like to support what we are doing regularly, to do so. Generosity is a key part of hospitality.

Messy Church and Breakfast Church both fit into a wide and diverse range of worship services on a Sunday, including a traditional 8.00 a.m. Communion service, 10.00 a.m. Holy Communion or Morning Worship, a 6.30 p.m. traditional evening service and an informal 7.00 p.m. service.

Our wider work with children and families includes an OFSTED-registered playgroup and two toddler groups (these groups see over 100 under-fives and their carers each week). There are also strong links with the church school as a number of church members volunteer in school, are school governors and work in the school too.

A Three-Dimensional Conclusion

Let's not depart this section too quickly. The real value will come when you examine your practice alongside what you have just read. A spot of reflection. You may want to do this exercise by yourself initially, but later on you should try it with your whole church team.

So, a two-part exercise. Take some time to think about the three dimensions:

- Your role as priest of your own home and the church's work in training parents to communicate to their own children, as well as your work helping parents perform their tasks better by the running of parenting courses and the like. All these are *bah'ith* activities.
- Your role in working with the church's children on Sundays and possibly small groups as well as communicating clearly that to be part of this community is a privilege that comes with responsibility. These are *mish-paw-khaw* activities.
- Your work with boys and girls who are not brought to church because their parents are not Christians; into this area we pitch our school's outreach, our children's clubs and our holiday events. But maybe also Messy Church (although it could be argued this is a *mish-paw-khaw* activity), and a whole range of creative events.

Part 1

In each of the three dimensions give yourself a mark out of ten, ten being the point where you couldn't do that particular area of ministry better. Now prayerfully look at your results in each of the three areas and ask yourself: How can I make all three dimensions rate a ten in my church and ministry? Then read on:

THE THREE DIMENSIONS

Bah'ith Working with your own children and equipping church families to communicate Jesus to their own children. Courses on being a Christian family, support for parents with teenagers, etc. Providing resources to help parents better communicate faith.

Mish-paw-khaw Communicating Jesus to the children of the church family and training others to do the same. Sunday children's ministry, intergenerational ministry, teaching the congregation that they are an example to children, etc.

Child evangelism Communicating Jesus to children who wouldn't hear that story in any other way. Schools, outreach projects, breakfast and homework clubs. And of course training others to do the same.

Part 2

This is the hard part. What would you need to do to make the scores a ten in each of the categories above?

The Fourth Dimension — You're It!

Remember all those wonderful sermons you've heard that tell you it's all about God? The ones with titles like "God is building His church". And the one stating, "Unless the Lord builds the house we labour in vain". I understand these messages. I get it. But I am a little concerned that they let us off the hook. There are also a whole pile of verses about being co-labourers with Christ, and of course Amos 3:7, "Surely the Sovereign Lord does nothing without revealing his plan to his servants the prophets" (NIV). The interference is that if nobody is listening, God isn't going to do it. And of course stirring passages where God is asking for people to stand in the gap for Him. A cry that Isaiah the prophet answers.

So yes, I get it, it's all about God. But if I may make the balancing statement. It's also all about you. Augustine puts it like this: "Pray as though everything depended on God. Work as though everything depended on you."

This section looks at the fourth dimension. You. God chooses to use people who make themselves available. Please hear that. Not the most gifted, or able or resourceful — just available. He can do the rest. And it's how He has always worked. If you are leading Israel out of captivity then you go and find a Moses, no matter how reluctant he is. If you are rebuilding, then you need a Nehemiah. If you are going to re-evangelize a nation you need a Robert Raikes and a George Wesley. If you're bringing revival to Wales you look for an Evan Roberts and maybe a Stephen and George Jeffries. If you are transforming China by the power of God then a Gladys Aylward or Hudson Taylor is a good choice; if India then maybe Amy Carmichael. You send a Jackie Pullinger to Hong Kong. But where you are right now. God commissions you. The task is straightforward enough. The re-evangelization of a community, a nation and a world. You.

Let's look a little closer at the amazing You!

None Greater

Luke chapter 1. The characters are Zechariah, a priest, and Elizabeth his wife. They are old and they have no children. Did you get that? "Old" and "barren". And God is about to give them a child. This is God being God. The God who does the impossible. If it's easy and within our ability then why should God show up? If you can do it in your own strength and ability and gift and it's worth doing, then go do it – why wait for God? He comes to do the things you and I simply could not do without Him. And remember this is just the warm-up, in a few verses we'll be introduced to a virgin who will also give birth to a child!

Let's keep going and check out what happens next.

Zechariah is on the worship rota. It's his turn to be in the temple. And an angel appears. And tells him that his old and barren wife is about to conceive and bear a son.

"Your wife Elizabeth will bear you a son, and you are to give him the name John."

And Zechariah asks a reasonable question:

"How can I be sure of this? I am an old man and my wife is well along in years."

But this is not a reasonable angel. He replies: "I am Gabriel. I stand in the presence of God, and I have been sent to speak to you."

Now don't miss this. That little statement tucked away in Luke 1 is the pattern for all ministry in whatever shape and form it might take. All ministry flows from the presence of God. If we haven't been in the presence of God, we have nothing to bring… no ministry! And this particular angel spends a lot of time there in the presence of God. We only read of three accounts of him in the whole Bible. And two of them are Luke 1 and Luke 2 (the other visit was hundreds of years earlier; to Daniel). Gabriel is created, he stands in the presence of the Lord and then from that position he steps out and changes the course of human history, and having done that, he returns to the presence of the Lord.

But as I mentioned. This is not a reasonable angel. And because

Zechariah didn't believe, he will not be able to speak until John is born. And then that delightful verse.

"When he came out, he could not speak to them. They realized he had seen a vision in the temple, for he kept making signs to them but remained unable to speak."

And there it is ladies and gentlemen. The first ever recorded game of charades!

And nine months pass. John is born and Zechariah gets to speak again.

But let's fast forward three decades or so.

There have been no words of scripture written for 400 years. There have been no prophetic voices in that same period. The land of Palestine where the drama unfolds has gone first from Persian control, to Alexandrian and then, most recently, to Roman occupation. The emperor Augustus has died and Tiberius, a debauched and brutish individual, climbs to the throne. There are three main political players: Pontius Pilate, the cruelly anti-Semitic Roman governor, and Herod and Phillip, the brothers who have inherited parts of Northern Palestine from their father Herod the Great.

So what will God do?

If you're asking that question, you've still not understood. He's already done it. The miracle happened three decades earlier, this is just the outworking. Watch what happens.

Darkness dominates.

And then onto history's stage walks John. This man is not the light; he is called to point to the light. He is the man who must blow the trumpet to proclaim the King, he's the man who must ring the bell to proclaim a change of government. The darkest night precedes the most glorious dawn. God has saved his best preacher for the darkest time.

But where has he been for thirty years? He has been in the presence of the Lord.

And there is so much more. But we need to jump. Although the end cannot be overlooked. The end of the story is shocking and wasteful and horrific. John is beheaded by an immoral king on the request of a spoilt girl and her immoral mother. It is a waste of human life. But he did what he came to do. Mark that. God's will is done. But it doesn't always end well.

But I want to go back a few chapters. I need to show you my favourite part. The Pharisees come and find John and they say to him: "Who are you? Are you the Christ? Are you the Elijah? Are you the prophet?" And John replies, "No." And so they press him. "Who are you?" "I am the voice in the wilderness proclaiming the way for the Lord."

But later, after the death of John, a similar conversation takes place. And Jesus asks them about John. And when they cannot answer, Jesus tells them that John was the prophet who was to come, he was the one who came in the spirit of Elijah.

Oh! That's awkward. A contradiction in Scripture.

John says he wasn't, Jesus says he was. That will cause some theological angst in New Testament studies.

How do we reconcile that?

Are you ready? Don't miss this: The most significant man ever to be born of a woman (Jesus' words). The one who came in the spirit of Elijah. The prophet. Didn't know it! He has no idea of his significance. There was no false humility on the part of John. He simply didn't know. And yet he did it anyway. He stood and he spoke and he proclaimed truth and he baptized.

And where's my proof? My proof is every time I address a room full of children and family workers. Every time I speak at a children's ministry conference. I stand on a stage and stare out at hundreds of men and women who change the lives of boys and girls. Who truly transform communities. Who were building the "big society" before it became a sound bite. Who enable and empower children to be everything God created them to be. A room full of significant people. And they never know. They don't realize their significance. And still they do what they do. They speak words of truth and life; they show the love of Jesus in the way they behave; they speak of a God who forgives. The God of compassion. The God of love. And all the time God is using them… using you… to usher in His ever-increasing Kingdom. And you didn't even know it. But you do it anyway. Rain or shine. You make a difference.

You really are that significant.

Thank you for being You.

Did I Mention You're it?

Are you getting it? When they told you that it wasn't all about you…
they lied! Let's move backwards a little from John and the New
Testament to Jacob at the start of the Old Testament to allow me to
make a few more points under the heading of it all being about you.

We are introduced to Jacob in Genesis 25; Isaac prayed for his wife
Rebekah because she was childless. The Lord answered her prayer and
Jacob is conceived. There is only one Jacob. He is unique. He is born at
the same time as his brother Esau. He is also unique.

Every new life is amazing. You are amazing. There is a Latin phrase,
"ex nihlo". It means "out of nothing". There was a time when you
didn't exist. Then God brought you out of nothing and made you. The
incredible you.

Psalm 139 makes it clear that God stitched us together in our
mother's womb; we are fearfully and wonderfully made.

To use my friend Jim Bailey's words:

> I am fearfully and wonderfully designed
> I got a brilliant body and I got a brilliant mind
> It's all been put together, I am one of a kind
> Fearfully and wonderfully designed
> Fearfully and wonderfully designed.[30]

Before the foundations of the world were laid, God was working on
Project You. There is a moment when we take our first breath on planet
Earth and there'll come a time when we'll take our last. And every
breath in between is a gift from God to the incredible you.

I hope you are hearing this. Because this is truth and the intrinsic
nature of truth is it sets people free. And if you're going to be the best
children's and family worker on the planet then you'll need to be free.

So you take your next breath and another. And every one of them is
a gift. A generous, extraordinary, mysterious, inexplicable gift. And you

---

30   Bailey, Jim, "This is Love", Daybreak Music/Elevation, 2006.

get to be responsible for every one of those gifts. Joshua Herschel, the philosopher, said this: "And above all, remember that the meaning of life is to build a life as if it were a work of art."[31]

Whoever you are and whatever you do, no one has ever lived your life with your particular challenges and possibilities – you haven't been attempted before. The amazing Doctor Who said it like this: "You know that in 900 years of time and space, I've never met anyone who wasn't important."

And of course Jacob has a twin brother. Who is a better hunter than Jacob, stronger than Jacob, more muscular and, by all accounts, more hairy.

The curse of spending all our time comparing ourselves with others. They have a bigger children and families' ministry with a bigger budget and a bigger office and a better gunge tank. Who cares? Who they are is not important.

We all have friends, colleagues, siblings who sail through life without effort. Who pass tests without study, who earn lots of money without seeming to do any work.

There is a lovely moment when Jesus is reunited with Peter in John 21 and Jesus asks, "Do you love me?" He asks three times and then gives Peter an insight into the way Peter would die. Peter doesn't want to face it – he wants to deflect – so to avoid the awkwardness he points to John and asks, "What about him?" Jesus responds quickly and almost harshly, "What is that to you."

Jesus wants Peter focused on Peter. Who they are is not the important part. Let's not spend our *gift* comparing what others have or, worse still, in trying to be someone else. Be who you are. As Rob Bell says, "We rob ourselves of immeasurable joy when we compare what we do know about ourselves with what we don't know about someone else."[32]

Jacob is clearly far from perfect. He talks Esau out of his birthright by selling him a bowl of soup. Then tricks his father into getting Esau's blessing. His name means "heel grabber". It carries the sense of his being a deceiver. And Jacob has to escape; he needs to run away to his uncle. And while he's alone and on his journey he comes to Bethel, and there he encounters God.

---

31   Herschel, A. J., *Moral Grandeur and Spiritual Audacity*, Farrar, Straus and Giroux, 1997, p. 412.
32   Bell, Rob, *How to Be Here*, London: HarperOne, 2016, p. 47.

He's alone. Children's and families' workers are never alone. They're hopeless at it. But God needs you alone because He needs to minister to you, to knock some of the rough edges away, to keep you centred on Jesus. Think retreat. You have to. Come away with God regularly.

Ask yourself the question, are you finding enough time to be alone with God? The simple reality is you can't take people where you haven't been. But when we meet with God, when we truly encounter, He embeds that spark of energy within us. Jacob meets with God and now the world lies open before him…

I believe that. There is nothing that is impossible for those who have encountered. The Hebrew language has an interesting expression, "Tikkun Olam" – the Jewish idea that creation is not yet complete and you and I get to work with God at the creation and recreation of the world. We get to be partners in this ongoing work of creation.

So let me show you where we've gone so far:

- you're it – life is a gift – every breath is a gift
- who *they* are isn't important
- you've been to that place of encounter – Bethel
- you have been given a blank sheet of paper – you can do anything!

Don't let cynicism sneak in. Remember the intrinsic nature of truth is that it sets people free. You need to be free. Free to dream. What is God calling you to do? Are you already doing it? There is always more.

And in passing, Bethel does not make Jacob into a saint. He's still going to get it wrong a few more times. Jacob goes through a roller coaster ride. He works seven years for Rachel, but ends up marrying Leah, and then works another seven years on the basis that he gets Rachel at the start of those years. And then Laban changes his wages again and again, but Jacob does something strange with the vegetation to ensure he ends up with the stronger livestock… all rather odd. But what is clear is Jacob is not perfect. **There are definitely still flaws. Encounter has not made him perfect.**

We're all a bit flawed, a bit broken, just like most of the biblical heroes. But God didn't choose you because you have no weaknesses; He chose you because you have some strength and you were available. And so you are imperfect, but God chose you, appointed you. You are so incredibly special and you are ready to do even more amazing things for Jesus. And now for my favourite part: **you could fail!**

aSo you failed. So what. Get back up. Let's start again. Let's learn and get back up. It's only failure. Rob Bell says, "This is the beautiful, counterintuitive, strange, unexpected, reliable mystery built into the fabric of creation that is at work every time we fail."[33] How gorgeous is that? You failed. But that's what being alive is about. You fail sometimes. Rob adds, "This work has brought me more joy than I could ever measure, and there are times when it was so excruciating and disorientating and agonising that I thought I was done."[34]

And I get it. I crashed quite spectacularly in 2016. No one gets a free pass from hurt and brokenness. There were moments when it felt the whole world was against me. But you should have watched as I got back up, dusted myself down, and faced the world again. A whole crowd of witnesses from Hebrews 11 were cheering. To use Theodore Roosevelt's much-used speech:

> It is not the critic who counts; not the man who points out how the strong man stumbles, or where the doer of deeds could have done them better. The credit belongs to the man who is actually in the arena, whose face is marred by dust and sweat and blood; who strives valiantly; who errs, who comes short again and again, because there is no effort without error and shortcoming; but who does actually strive to do the deeds; who knows great enthusiasms, the great devotions; who spends himself in a worthy cause; who at the best knows in the end the triumph of high achievement, and who at the worst, if he fails, at least fails while daring greatly, so that his place shall never be with those cold and timid souls who neither know victory nor defeat.[35]

So I walked back in to that place of sweat and blood. We're not designed to be the critic. Leave that to others. We belong in the arena.

So let's stay in the arena and let's stay engaged. And that isn't as easy as it sounds. Most twenty-first-century people are not there! I'd best explain that. I'm in a middle of a conversation with you but I can

---

33   Bell, *How to Be Here*, p. 126.
34   *Bell, How to Be Here*, p. 69.
35   www.theodore-roosevelt.com/images/research/speeches/maninthearena.pdf

see that you are miles away, thinking about later or earlier, but definitely not here. We go for lunch and I talk and I'm sure I'm interesting, but you constantly look down to the mobile phone in front of you on the table waiting for that text message which is clearly going to be more interesting than me. I am going to start taking a hammer to lunch so when that phone goes beep I can smash it to a thousand pieces – none of them saying, "I love you". You play with the children but with one eye on the phone and a mind far, far away. You eat dinner with the family but you are rehearsing conversations for the morning. STOP!

"Just this." (That's the expression I stole from one of Rob Bell's friends). "Just this." When my mind wanders, I bring it back and I say to myself right now I am doing *just this*. When I am playing ball with my sons, I say *just this*. Someone else can answer the phone. Someone else can worry about tomorrow. I'm here. Right now. Just this.

And that takes discipline. Develop set times for dealing with emails. Build proper rhythm into the week. Run in the afternoon. Stop work at 4 p.m. Take that extra day off for you. Take another day for research. Write in your time sheet, "Was working with God at the creation and recreation of the world."

So summary so far:

- You're it – life is a gift – every breath is a gift.
- Who *they* are isn't important.
- You've been to that place of Encounter – Bethel.
- You've been given a blank sheet of paper – you can do anything!
- God didn't choose you because you have no weakness. But because you have some strength.
- You could fail. But failure is overrated.
- Be here. Just this.

And that'll get you through, and you'll be better than most. But there is another level. But to get there you'll need to wrestle. Jacob eventually flees from Laban and once again he finds himself alone. It's not a coincidence. Alone is important. His wives and children and workers and livestock have gone ahead. He's going back to his home. But first he comes to Mahanaim. It's the place of two camps. It's the place where Jacob will choose. He's good, way above average. But there is more. But he doesn't have to go there.

And now in that place of aloneness. God comes. And they wrestle. It is painful. Sometimes excruciatingly so. It involves huge effort and physical and emotional resources. And for us, unlike the Jacob account, very rarely is it over in one night; sometimes it can be months or even years. But the result of that night of wrestling is the person is irrevocably changed. Literally in this account. Jacob walked differently. This is Peniel. Jacob sees God face to face. He will walk differently.

We need all our children's and families' workers to encounter God at Bethel. But we need more and more who are prepared to go further. To see God face to face. Job wrote, "I had heard about you, but now I have seen you." To get close to God and minister from that position we need generals and apostles in children's and familes' ministry. Will you go there? And in that place God changes Jacob's name. Jacob, you will remember, means "heel grabber". From now on he will be called "Israel". Israel means "Prince of God".

What Do You See?

Many years ago now I was asked to go to Manchester to speak to a team of young people who had taken a year out to work with churches up and down the country. The team was together for a couple of days and I had been asked to go and speak to them about ministry to children. I set out relatively early, giving myself enough time to get to Manchester. It was only when I was 10 km outside Manchester that it dawned on me that other than the fact that the training day was in Manchester and I was due to start speaking at 11 a.m., I didn't know any more about the location of the training day – unfortunately this is not unusual behaviour for me!

Vision

The point I am making is this. When I set out early on that day all I needed to know was the area where I was heading. I didn't need the detail. It was only when I was getting close to the actual area that I needed detail. Vision is not unlike this. God rarely shows us the whole picture at once. He just shows us a couple of steps so that we can start. If you are waiting for the whole picture you will never start. You need an overview vision that as Habakkuk 2:2 says can be written down: "Then the Lord told me: 'I will give you my message in the form of a vision. Write it clearly enough to be read at a glance.'"

Your vision can be as simple as, "I will run the largest children's club in my city." This is not an arrogant vision, by the way. Our vision is supposed to be big. We must attempt things so amazing that unless God steps in we will end up flat on our faces. We must aim high. We serve a God of creativity, who spoke and the world came into being. Who took dust and "fearfully and wonderfully" (Psalm 139:14) formed you and me. Let's dream big dreams; let's do some amazing, exciting things for Jesus.

An American company called General Electric (GE) has this mission statement: "To build, move, power and cure the world." Their moto is:

"If we can dream it we can do it."

Can you imagine what would happen if some people who are committed to the expansion of the Kingdom of God got hold of that sort of philosophy and made it part of their everyday living? Former NASA geologist, Michael Duke, had an even better one: "The possibilities are limited only by our imagination and determination, and not by the physics."

Let's dream some dreams. Let's make God famous.

> COMMENT: Our minds are rarely tuned into what God is saying. Sometimes God gives us a vision and we say, "God, that is too big, how can I possibly do that?" We forget what God can do through us; we forget that we must not try to outwork God-given vision in our own strength. But equally we may get a vision from God and are tempted to say – "Is that it?" God's ways are not our ways and sometimes our little club of ten may have in it ten apostles. It may seem small, but we rarely understand God's economy. The key is very simple. Listen to God and do what you're told!

Goals

There it is, we have begun – now we must prayerfully break it down. We need a venue, we need some people to help, we need to choose the best night, and we need some finance. We have now moved into the area of goals. The things we need to do to outwork the vision. At this stage we don't know which children we are going to reach, we don't know what sort of teaching we are going to use, we don't actually know if we are going to be teaching at all. Maybe it's a football club God wants us to run!

Now as we move closer we need more detail. When I was 10 km from Manchester that day, I had to make a few frantic phone calls to find out the detail. Needless to say, I arrived with almost thirty seconds to spare! But at this stage the detail does become important. We need to know if it is going to be a football club. Is it a project to help Christian children? Is it an outreach project to give us the opportunity to be spiritual foster parents?

The much-used acrostic to help us set goals is the word "SMART".

Our goals must be:

Specific   What exactly are we looking to achieve? For example, to start a new club in Ourtown school hall?

Measurable   How many people will it bring in; how many new leaders will we have?

Achievable   Can this really be done? Yes, there is faith involved but if the Seventh Day Adventists use it all week then we won't be able to use Ourtown school hall.

Reviewable   We have said it will happen in six months; three months in it is clear it isn't going to, so let's review and refocus.

Time-related   How long will it take to complete this particular goal?

Goals allow us to strategically outwork the vision. I may have a vision to run the largest children's church in my city, but it will be strategic goal-setting that will get me there. I will need to set goals: after six months I will have fifty children and four staff; after twelve months I will have seventy-five and five leaders, and so on.

COMMENT: Remember to allow God to take your thinking outside the box. All over our nation, and our world for that matter, people are enjoying great success with the open-air children's club. The programme runs exactly the same as that outlined in the Beginner's Guide section, except it takes place outside. The children sit on sheets of plastic in two or three teams and sing their songs, play their games, and listen to the preaching. Registration can still happen, visitation can still happen, wider invites to community activities can still happen. I stood in the South Bronx, New York City once and watched as two people presented the teaching programme to just over 500 children from a low trailer with the help of a couple of volunteers. To make life more interesting a knife fight broke out beside them.

CONT: The man who was teaching told the children to keep their eyes firmly fixed on him and they did. Open-air children's clubs are particularly appropriate for those cities where there are huge numbers of street kids. Clearly UK weather doesn't lend itself to this style of outreach for much of the year. Many very successful clubs in the UK bus the children to the venue. This clearly has difficulties, but it has been proven to work in both rural and urban areas. As I mentioned earlier, I have usually preferred to avoid using buses and focus instead on the children on our doorstep (that is, those within a couple of miles of the church).

Perseverance and burden

Jesus said in Luke 9:62, "Anyone who starts ploughing and keeps looking back isn't worth a thing to God's kingdom." You can have the strongest burden and the most amazing vision, but if you don't have perseverance it really isn't worth much. The ability to see things through has become a lost art. So many people quit just before the miracle happens. If it were easy, it wouldn't be worth doing. It's supposed to cost us something.

Let me illustrate with a narrative from 2 Chronicles 14:1–10:

Abijah died and was buried in Jerusalem. Then his son Asa became king, and Judah had ten years of peace.

Asa obeyed the Lord his God and did right. He destroyed the local shrines and the altars to foreign gods. He smashed the stone images of gods and cut down the sacred poles used in worshiping the goddess Asherah. Then he told everyone in Judah to worship the Lord God, just as their ancestors had done, and to obey his laws and teachings. He destroyed every local shrine and incense altar in Judah.

The Lord blessed Judah with peace while Asa was king, and so during that time, Asa fortified many of the towns. He said to the people, "Let's build walls and defence towers for these towns, and put in gates that can be locked with bars. This land still belongs to us, because we have obeyed the Lord our God. He has given us peace from all our enemies." The people did everything Asa had suggested.

> Asa had a large army of brave soldiers: Three hundred thousand of them were from the tribe of Judah and were armed with shields and spears; two hundred eighty thousand were from Benjamin and were armed with bows and arrows.

> Zerah from Ethiopia led an army of a million soldiers and three hundred chariots to the town of Mareshah in Judah. Asa met him there, and the two armies prepared for battle in Zephathah Valley.

The story starts off very positively. A righteous king who undoes the bad things his father had set in place. Asa places God back into his rightful position and the whole nation looks well. Then Zerah from Ethiopia decided to visit – this was not a social call, it was war. And to make life worse, Asa is in a valley (having grown up in one I'm an expert on valleys). Asa could not back out – if he took his men up the mountain and out of the valley then the Ethiopians would pick them off from behind.

Vision runs the same route – it must. All starts off well, everything seems to be coming together nicely, then Zerah visits, the money runs out, a key person leaves, you hit a low attendance week, the school won't let you in any more. Zerah comes.

In this story we learn a lot about what to do when Zerah comes. Firstly it is worth noting that humanly speaking all was lost – Asa was overwhelmed and outnumbered. He wasn't being pessimistic; he was being real. He knew that he couldn't win this one in his own strength.

What an incredibly refreshing place to come to. To know that by ourselves we are lost. That by ourselves we are outnumbered and overwhelmed. It really is not wrong to end up in this position; it isn't this that decides the outcome, it's the next bit – what we do next. What our response is to the situation – not the situation itself. All the great men of God found themselves here. Paul said that in Asia he despaired even of life itself; Moses looked at a burning bush and couldn't understand why he should go; David uttered the words in Psalm 55, "God if I was a dove I would fly far away from here."

Asa's responses are illuminating and noteworthy. He does two things. Firstly, he responds naturally; he does what he can do. He lines his armies up. Our natural response might be to ask the treasurer for more money, to make an appeal for more leaders, to talk to the local council about a new hall or just to take a nap! But Asa also responded supernaturally. He prayed and in doing so he reveals to us the key – the way to make perseverance possible. He involved God in the battle. He invited God in and that would make all the difference. Asa prayed, "God only with you can a powerless army defeat a greater one."

He invited God in and it all changed. It always does. In 2 Corinthians Paul said, "God's power is made perfect in weakness."

Moses once afraid stood before Pharaoh and commanded him to let God's people go.

And of David, who wanted to fly away, One of Absalom the rebel's advisors comments, "Don't go after your father now, for he is a fighter."

That's the sort of testimony we're looking for. People who persevere, people who don't give in before the job is complete, people who even their enemies will say of them that they are fighters. We must keep going and we must keep God involved, for when God is involved we become brave in danger, cheerful in monotony and positive in the face of discouragement.

Mary Shelley's story *Frankenstein* is very interesting, although the plot is very simplistic – a genius but mad scientist creates a person from lots of body parts and then artificially brings it to life. The person turns out to be a monster. The monster then upsets some villagers who pursue the monster to a Gothic castle where they burn the castle and the kill the monster. As well as providing generations of film makers with material, the story is also an astute insight into the futility of humanism – what happens when we leave God out of the equation and try and put together a programme by borrowing lots of components from elsewhere: we create a monster and it all ends in disaster. God must never be left out of the equation! This can't be done with off-the-shelf products from around the world.

The outcome of the Asa story is very encouraging (2 Chronicles 14:12–14):

The Lord helped Asa and his army defeat the Ethiopians. The enemy soldiers ran away, but Asa and his troops chased them as far as Gerar. It was a total defeat – the Ethiopians could not even fight back!

> The soldiers from Judah took everything that had belonged to
> the Ethiopians. The people who lived in the villages around Gerar
> learned what had happened and were afraid of the Lord.

God made us a promise: "In this world you will have trouble" (John 16:33).

He then attached a commandment: "Don't be afraid, I've overcome the world."

But before we depart this chapter, allow me to introduce one more layer to our **Burden, Vision, Goals, Perseverance** formula, and that is the **Culture**. Brené Brown quotes the truism: "CULTURE EATS STRATEGY FOR BREAKFAST".[36]

In the last decade I have learned the power of that. The rest can be perfect: right goals, right strategies, but if your culture is wrong, then it will eventually come tumbling down. In this context I would define *culture* as *the stuff you and your team live in*. Is it a positive culture, is it a negative culture, is it a harsh culture, is it an empowering culture, is it a restrictive culture? What does your culture look like? I run with four cultural statements; they colour everything else. The first three are:

- **Everyone is important and significant.** You would have picked up my feelings on this from the last chapter.
- **Everyone has a part to play.**
- **The job of employed staff is to equip and empower others.**

It's hard to express how important that point is. Too many churches fall into the trap of paying someone to come and do the kids' ministry so they don't have to. It will not work. The whole body of Christ must function. Employed staff are there to equip and empower others. Your church council/board/deacons/governing body need to be clear on that when they appoint, otherwise it will all unravel.

Let's put this another way. Ephesians 2 weaves together the strings of Ephesians 1. We read in Ephesians 2 that we are God's handiwork created for good works in Christ. We are God's handiwork – not maybe, not one day you will be, but *you are* God's handiwork, created for good works in Christ. People are God's greatest resource, far too significant

---

36   Brown, Brené, *Daring Greatly*, London, Penguin, 2015, p. 174.

not to take up their part in the body of Christ. And in light of that, the job of leadership is simply to ensure that they are aware of this. Aware and playing their part.

I recently watched a documentary on the Discovery Channel called, *Starlings on Otmoor*. You can dig out the clip on YouTube. In early evening during the winter months, thousands of starlings gather in the trees around Otmoor near Oxford in the UK. And in the documentary, the commentator says this:

> The starlings quit feeding and take to the air and gather in large flocks of up to a thousand... I've spent hours watching and never seen a collision. How can that be possible? Individuals, but moving in a single identity.[37]

Followers of Jesus disagree at times, but we are wired to fly together – each with different gifts, interweaving, interlocking, some fly higher, some further, some faster, some with a more elaborate flight path, but together we make the most extraordinary patterns in the sky and we never collide... wow! Ephesians 4 tells us God gave some to be apostles, some prophets and evangelists, some pastors and teachers, some with the ministry of hospitality, some with the gift of administration. Apostles who break open new ground. Prophets who are strategists, visionaries, seeing a little further. Evangelists who are great proclaimers of truth, whether on a large stage or to the postman! Pastors who care and listen and help. Teachers who present complex truth in digestible forms...

The body of Christ is packed full of these amazing gifts. And therefore the job of leadership is quite simply to keep you flying, reaching your potential, being everything you were created to be – an active part of the body of Christ. Leaders are not to skim in and out of clouds proclaiming how great we are, but instead to help others to soar.

And the fourth cultural statement?

- **We believe in growth, numerically through evangelism, and spiritually through discipleship.**

I call this our "warrior spirit". The desire to grow. Don't miss this. Resources and structure and coaching is all in vain if there's no warrior

---

37   www.youtube.com/watch?v=RInNt0UsLNM

spirit that says we can grow. You see it again and again in the sporting world: two equally matched individuals, or two equally matched teams, the same resources, the same structure, the same leadership, but one of them wants it just a little bit more – a determination to win. A warrior spirit. We can grow. It is the most natural thing for us to do.

If there's no warrior spirit, then it's all in vain. If there's no desire to win, then defeat is imminent. And so very often the church doesn't look as if it wants to win. It sometimes doesn't even recognize what it's fighting for.

We exist to sound a clear and distinct message. To proclaim God. The church is God's primary vehicle for changing the world. Our children's club, our family ministry, our Messy Church, our Sunday school, our small groups for teenagers. They exist to change the world. In 1882 Frederick Booth Tucker of the Salvation Army went to win India for Jesus. He took with him three ladies armed with tambourines and he played a tuba. They were sent to prison on numerous occasions for breaching the peace, but eventually they would see thousands of Indians become Christians and set up numerous social regeneration projects across India.

What sort of people set out to convert a nation with a tuba and three tambourines? Those with a warrior spirit.

One of my favourite "Star Trek" legends is the account of how James T. Kirk became the only Starfleet cadet to beat the Kobayashi Maru simulation. The Kobayashi Maru is supposed to be the ultimate test, the no-win scenario. A Starfleet vessel surrounded by Klingon Warbirds with no chance of victory. No possibility of success. It tests how you respond in a no-win scenario. It's not supposed to be a test of strategy, but of character. But James T. Kirk doesn't believe there is such a thing as a no-win scenario. And he does the only thing that can possibly beat the simulation... he reprograms the computer.[38]

I have been to so many meetings recently where the subject has been, "What do we do about the projections of falling attendance and how can we best reduce the overall numbers of ministers?" But I sit in these gatherings and I simply ask: **"It's not compulsory though is it? Declining congregations are not compulsory! We can grow."**

---

38   A lot of attention is paid to this in J. J. Abrams' 2009 remake of the Star Trek movie.

My comments are invariably greeted with surprise, sometimes with humour (the assumption being that I couldn't possibly be serious). As if nobody had considered that option before. We are so used to buying into the statistical projections of dwindling church numbers that we forget that the no-win scenario doesn't need to be our reality. We can reprogram the computer. And I desperately think that our churches may need some reprograming.

We need to believe that we can grow. With the right people, the right structures, the right leaders and with a warrior spirit, we can see churches grow and recognize again that they are God's primary vehicle for changing our world.

Graham Kendrick's song "God Put a Fighter in Me" is now so old it is new! But let me remind you of the words:

Where have all the Christian soldiers gone?
Where is the resistance?
Will no one be strong?
When will we stand up tall and straight,
Rise up and storm the gate.

How can we fail to get excited,
The battle is ours, why don't we fight it?
Battalions of darkness rise above me, but
God put a fighter in me, put a fighter in me.[39]

The battle is ours, and it is very winnable. The re-evangelization of a nation really is possible. A mission to change the world isn't supposed to be the domain of Unilever, or GE or NASA... It's ours.

---

39   Graham Kendrick, Make Way Music, 1978.

There's Only One Real Key

David had been journeying long and hard. He had led his men valiantly. He had lived with incredible standards of integrity and righteousness. He had always done the right thing. Yet he had just returned from the journey, hoping to come back to his wife and children, hoping for a time of rest and relaxation before he continued on. Then suddenly, as he rode into camp, he saw smoke billowing high into the air. It was his camp. Ziklag was on fire. His possessions were in flames. As he came closer the enormity of the situation hit him. Not only were all his possessions on fire, his wife and children and everything he and his men owned were gone.

And, as if the situation couldn't get any worse, now his friends – those he had helped, those he had encouraged when they were downcast and depressed, those whom he had carried when they couldn't support themselves – those self-same men now wanted to kill him. They wanted to stone their leader to death.

David was facing one of his bleakest moments. He had entered a dark time – a time that we are not immune from; a defining moment in his life. Several weeks after this episode David would ride triumphantly into Jerusalem and would be crowned king. He would prove to be the greatest king Israel would ever have outside King Jesus himself. But before he gets to Jerusalem, he must get through Ziklag.

Ziklag is that defining moment which enables us to move onto that level way above average, or it can be the moment when we decide that mediocrity is where we will live our lives. It is the central base around which all else hinges. It is David's final test before kingship. If he passes this test then he will walk on into triumph and glory; if he fails this test the shepherd boy will at best return to his sheep, at worse will die.

David's past was incredibly exciting. He had been anointed king by Samuel the prophet and he had defeated Goliath. He had gathered to himself men and women who were depressed, discouraged, in debt and desperate and David had made them great. But now he faces the defining moment.

We all come there. We must. Anyone worth anything in God's kingdom must pass the Ziklag test. They must prove faithful under intense pressure; they must be made of sufficient metal that they don't shrink away at the first sign of opposition. Allow me to make some general observations on David's predicament that may help us also:

- The decision was his: God willed for him to get up and sort the situation but He would never override His special gift to mankind; He would never override free will. The decision here was David's and David's alone.
- He was on his own, nobody was going to help him up. He had no:
- physical support; his men were not going to support or help him – on the contrary they wanted to kill him
- material support; all his material possessions had been taken
- emotional support; his wife and children had been taken away; his emotional shelter was gone.

It so happens that there's not always someone there to help you up, and sometimes God designs it that way. Stripped of everything, what will David do?

- Those he had worked with, those he had strengthened and encouraged, now wanted to stone him. Anyone who has ever held a position of responsibility will understand the emotions that this brings up. I've certainly been there a few times.

I genuinely believe that we must all face that place of Ziklag, that place where two different futures open up before us. And for everyone who comes through to be a king I wonder how many return to being shepherds. Having destiny is not enough; being prophesied over is not enough. Many people have destiny but may never see it fulfilled.

It would be true to say that 90 per cent of our life is governed by our decisions and only 10 per cent by unforeseen circumstances. However, I think it is our response and our decision process within the 10 per cent that defines us – that decision in the unforeseen circumstance, that decision when we feel devoid of everything, that decision in the Ziklag time that makes the difference.

The times when nobody wants to support our vision to reach boys and girls for Jesus, that time when nobody wants to work with us, that time when we are physically and emotionally drained. Dragging ourselves out week after week, through those cold autumnal evenings and those depressing winter nights to do what we are convinced God called us to do. And to learn that in those times it is God Himself who destines us to be devoid of support. But it is so important that God allows us to go through these times for ultimately it is the builder that defines the shape of the building. If God can get His builders right then there is no real issue when it comes to what they build. Paul built as a wise master builder. It was going to be good and healthy and full of God because that was what Paul was like. The builder defines the shape.

And David was always going to prove himself at Ziklag. Sun Tze, known as a sixth-century BC Chinese general, is commonly said to be the author of *The Art of War*. In it, he comments that victories are won before the battles begin. And David had been through many tests that prepared him for Ziklag. At the time the other tests must have seemed difficult, but they all prepared the man of God for the next rung of the ladder. So let's see what we can learn from David.

• He had an open and honest relationship with God
David wasn't just praying liturgical prayers that he had memorized; David had cultivated an open and honest relationship with the creator of the universe. He told God how he felt.

• He knew about the power of praise
Psychologists are only just beginning to realize the potential of music to change our moods and emotions; David knew more than this. He knew that God himself inhabited the praise of His people and through praise David could lift his feelings, his emotions and his spirit and position himself to overcome in every situation.

• He knew how to draw power from outside himself
New Age gurus talk of our need to draw power from within, to draw strength from something mystical inside us. (It is almost certainly a distortion of the Ecclesiastes teaching that eternity has been hidden in our hearts.) But David knew that it wasn't mystical power from within that he needed, but instead supernatural power from without. He needed to draw strength from his God as he had done so many times in the past.

If we can build these principles very firmly into our lives *before the battle* – then we will always be successful and live our lives on a level way above average. Let us remember the sobering thought that for every person who goes on to be king, there are many who return to being a shepherd. To change this generation of boys and girls we desperately need some people who will operate on a level way above average and I believe that God is raising those people up right now. But they must first pass through Ziklag.

Catherine Booth was the wife of General William Booth, the founder of the Salvation Army. Catherine was struggling with the idea of joining her husband as he travelled in the nineteenth century throughout the UK and beyond to share the gospel. Catherine had seen William being verbally and physically abused as he stood outside public houses preaching. She saw bottles thrown at him and the constant torment that he endured as he saw men and women won to Jesus. Catherine decided to commit the whole thing to God in prayer, and she knelt and began to pray.

The story goes that as she prayed Jesus himself appeared before her in a vision. She asked Jesus if there were another way. Jesus held up his nail-pierced hands as if to indicate that sometimes His way was a way of suffering. Catherine bowed her head and then asked, "Then Lord, will you be with me?" Jesus answered, "Until the end of time." In the strength of these words Catherine stood and joined her husband, boldly proclaiming the gospel.

Sometimes to follow Jesus involves sacrifice and suffering. There never was a guarantee that it would be easy, but if we can keep going and build the right principles into our lives and never give up then we can make amazing things happen. We have a promise from Jesus himself, "I will be with you always, even until the end of this age" (Matthew 28:20, NCV).

Allow me to visit that same medicine, but place it in a different bottle. This is the story of Gladys Aylward. It's one of my favourites.

One Saturday in 1932, Gladys Aylward left London's Liverpool Street station for the long train ride across Europe and Russia; God had told her to go to China and to China she was going.

Gladys was one of those whose lives had been touched by God. She knew what it was to have a life touched by Jesus himself. It made her spectacular. She had to be asked to leave theological college because they had suggested she was not clever enough to be a missionary. She may have been told that she would never be able to go to China, but she didn't believe it. She knew who Jesus was and he had changed her life.

People may have said no, but she was going anyway. God had said yes.

Gladys worked in various jobs and saved up her wages. Then she heard of a 73-year-old missionary called Jeannie Lawson, who happened to be looking for a younger woman to carry on her missionary work in China. Gladys wrote to Jeannie, who in turn told her that if she could make it to China then Gladys could stay with her and work with her. So, on 15 October, Gladys set off from London with nothing but her passport, her Bible, her ticket, and just over two pounds, bound for China.

The journey was far from easy. The first difficulty was in travelling through Germany where officials were not happy when they asked Gladys why she was going to China. "God said," she simply replied.

They asked her many questions. They tried to stop her continuing but there was no way this lady was turning back. But the worst was yet to come.

She travelled on through Russia. At that time the Russians were at war with China and this particular part of the journey was very hazardous. At one point, at a place called Chita, the train stopped and soldiers boarded the train, commanding everyone to get off. But Gladys protested. Her ticket said Dairen (now Dalian), a place on the China Sea (now the Yellow Sea), and she would not get off until she arrived there. The train continued. But some miles later the train was stopped again and this time the conductor announced that the train would not go any further for several months.

Gladys had no choice but to get off the train and walk back to Chita. It was a long walk and before long the night had come and with it the blistering cold. She stopped to rest under a tunnel. In the background she could hear the sounds of wolves howling in the Russian countryside. Wolves coming closer, but as it turned out the morning came before the wolves and she continued on to Chita. At Chita she boarded another train and despite a long argument with another soldier, she insisted on being taken to Dairen. The train continued on but no further than Vladivostok.

In Vladivostok the secret police interrogated her and would certainly have locked her in prison if a stranger hadn't helped her escape to the harbour. At the harbour she tried to get a ship to Japan, but the captain refused to take her because she had no money. She pleaded with him until eventually he agreed to take her.

From Japan to Tientsin, and then by train, then bus, then mule, to the inland city of Yangchen, in the mountainous province of Shansi, a little south of Peking (Beijing). Most of the residents had seen no Europeans other than Jeannie Lawson, and now Gladys.

The college principal had said NO, but God said YES.

The Germans had said NO, but Gladys kept going because God said YES.

The Russians had said NO but Gladys kept going because God said YES.

The wolves had tried to stop her but God had said YES.

The Secret Service had tried to stop her but God said YES.

Even the China Sea had tried to stand in her way, but this was a life touched by God; this was a life that Jesus had made spectacular – nothing would, or could, stop her.

Gladys would do what God had told her to do. This was a spectacular lady. God was going to do amazing things through her. A spectacular life. A life that would never be content on the mole hill; this was a life destined for Everest. Gladys stood at just five feet tall. She was not intelligent by the world's measure of intelligence. She simply did what God had asked. And therein lies the key.

She simply did what God had asked, and she kept going.

SECTION 2
Communication

Learning A New Language

He who learns to communicate to a generation ultimately has the power to control that generation. And while we need to be very clear that for us it is not about control (control is something the devil wants to do to people, but it violates one of God's greatest gifts to us: free will), we do need to influence the generation. And to influence this generation for godliness and righteousness involves communicating well. After all, if God has called us to children's work then our very vocation is communication. He has gifted us and sent us to communicate the good news about His Kingdom and about a God who unconditionally loves.

When we want to chop a tree down, there is very little use hitting the tree harder and harder if the axe itself is blunt. What we need to do is sharpen the axe.

On a recent visit to a restaurant in France it was interesting to watch a particularly arrogant Englishman trying to order his food. He clearly had no knowledge of French and the waitress for her part had very little knowledge of English. The man wanted chips with his meal instead of the potatoes that came as standard. He asked the waitress repeatedly for "chips" and when she continued to look blank at him he began to shout the word "chips" at her very loudly. The waitress, instead of suddenly realizing what the man wanted because he was now shouting louder, was now looking around desperately for a policeman to rescue her from the mad Englishman.

I am unsure where the idea came from, but somewhere locked away in our psyche is a theory that says if we are not being understood then we need to raise the volume. Many of us may have experienced similar events in our churches: when the preacher sees blank faces staring back at him he begins to shout his message in an attempt to be understood! Unfortunately, it doesn't work. If we would like to be understood, then we need to speak in a language that is understandable and not simply raise the volume – this will have the exact opposite effect.

When it comes to communication with children the goal must surely not be harder and louder, but sharper and clearer. To be able to influence this generation we must be understood; we must communicate well. But before we jump in, allow me to interject with the warning, "The Father who sent me has commanded me what to say and how to say it" (John 12:49, NLT).

Clearly Jesus is our best example of a great communicator, but He is telling us that He only speaks what the Father has told Him to, and in the way that the Father had told Him.

So two clear points can be drawn from this verse:

- the Father tells us what to say
- the Father tells us how to say it.

So the Father gives us the message and, just as important, he also gives us the method of delivery. With that in mind let's move on.

Here is the format for the first fifteen minutes of a particular episode of *Sesame Street*:

- Elmo going to meet Prince Charming
- Titles
- Elmo meets prince but he's on the cell phone
- Elmo meets prince but he's on the fax
- Elmo meets prince but he's on the normal phone
- Elmo meets prince but he's on the answer phone
- Prince Charming is stressed and resigns
- Video – telephone ringing in street
- Animation – talking, walking telephone
- Video – two children make a map of neighbourhood and then explain their map
- Animation – the letter "k" – kangaroo, kite, etc.
- Video – the city garden project
- Puppets – dance and rap
- Humans chatting about poems
- Interview – Big Bird meets a poet – what is a poem, a game with words
- Animation – toothpaste
- Video – how to clean your teeth
- Animation – I love my teeth
- Song – toothbrush song

Nineteen different components in only fifteen minutes of television. The longest item was the title sequence itself. *Sesame Street* is aimed at a pre-school audience.

And then we come to our children's club for which we have prepared well, and we have an excellent story, an excellent talk, and excellent object lesson, and the children just don't seem interested – they are fidgety, they whisper to each other, they pull each other's hair. We think we have failed, but it's not us. We think they are rude and just plain naughty, but it's not them. From pre-school onwards this generation has learned to digest information in small pieces, presented in different ways and presented very quickly. They would love to listen to your story, they would love to give you their full attention, but since pre-school they have been taught to enjoy the fast-moving, constantly changing programme. They would love to listen, but they don't know how.

I visited a school recently which, at the same time was, for one week, being inspected (I am invited in to take assemblies at many schools when the inspectors are visiting – I am beginning to suspect it is no coincidence).[40] I took the assembly and talked to the 300 children at the school, who are aged from four to eight. I managed to have a quick conversation with one of the inspectors at the end and asked how the school was doing. Her response was revealing. She told me that like most schools up and down the country the children were struggling to sit still for more than five minutes.

This is an entertainment-based culture. Today's children enjoy being involved and love experimenting, but they need their information in bite-sized parcels.

The part the inspector was struggling with was how I had managed to hold 300 children's attention for twenty-five minutes by just standing at the front and talking. I smiled and told her that I practised a lot. The truth is, I know a secret. I know how this generation digest information. **I know that to be listened to you have to present a spiritual diet containing all the essential food groups, but package it so that it looks like a Big Mac™.** I told a story and into that story I wove other stories. I said the same thing in several ways. But a bit more on stories in the next chapter.

There are two fundamental systems of communication:

---

40   Particularly when they are week-long inspections!

1. Deductive communication

This is based on linear logic and is the type primarily taught by our theological colleges. It usually involves an introduction, three points and a conclusion. If I were to talk about "love" using this type of communication then I would do it as follows:

- **Introduction:** Today I am going to talk about love and I will touch on three Greek words associated with it:
- Part 1   *Phileo* Love
- Part 2   *Eros* Love
- Part 3   *Agape* Love
- **Conclusion:** Today we talked about love and the three Greek words associated with it.

The problem with this is simple. As soon as children know the ending they no longer feel the need to listen, so as soon as they discover from the introduction that there are three Greek words for love they no longer feel the need to listen and therefore don't at all.

2. Inductive communication

Induction is entertainment-based. In this method people are drawn into the presentation and don't know where the end is until it arrives. If we were to show a structure it would look something like:

- **Attention:** Grab the audience's attention (if this doesn't happen in the first thirty seconds it is not going to happen).
- **Interest**: Keep the audience interested.
- **Conviction:** Draw the audience to the conclusion showing them how it applies to them.
- **Response:** Never let the audience go without giving them opportunity to respond in one way or another.

If I were to talk about love using this method of communication I might borrow an idea from someone who was really good at it, "A man was going down from Jerusalem to Jericho and fell into the hands of robbers..." (Luke 10:30, NRSV).

Jesus, the master communicator, communicated inductively. Our theological colleges rarely list Jesus as a great preacher. He doesn't fit the modern preaching paradigm. Yet He was an amazing communicator

– so much so that the people of the day would travel for miles to hear Him. And he could hold the attention of all ages at the same time and in the same place. However, when we look at His style and technique we soon discover that *Sesame Street* isn't so original after all. Jesus' Sermon on the Mount was approximately eighteen minutes long, yet into that eighteen minutes Jesus packs 348 different images and experiences from everyday life. He says "you" (as opposed to some people) 221 times, and He used comedy.

We must learn to let our programmes evolve, but understand the need for fast-moving, magazine-style content. We must have the confidence to try different things and not be overly concerned if they fail dismally. Out of ten programme items, only five may work. That is not a problem: when we start the following week we know we have five items that work well. We must never be afraid of making mistakes. As one entrepreneur put it, "If we don't make mistakes, we'll never make anything."[41] We should never be afraid of making mistakes; we should only fear the absence of creative, constructive and corrective responses to those mistakes. If you talk to any experienced children's worker they will be able to list a whole catalogue of mistakes that they have made as they travelled their journey from average to expert. Remember, experts are hewn out of the bedrock of experience, and it's rare that all experiences are positive.

Having spent some time talking about the method of presenting the message, it is important to state that it really doesn't matter at the end of the day how good the method of presentation is or how good the message is if the messenger is somehow flawed. We think our battle is in the area of apologetics – what we say. It's not. **Children are not so much interested in what we say as in who we are**. The statistics speak for themselves:

When we communicate:

- 15 per cent of our message is to do with content.
- 25 per cent of our message is to do with tone.
- 60 per cent of our message is to do with who we are.

When I stand in front of a group of children and speak, my message only amounts to 15 per cent of my overall communication. If my tone

---

41   Chesterton, G. K., The Return of Don Quixote, Cornwall: House of Stratus, 1927.

is not consistent with my message, for example if I tell the children that God loves them, but my tone is sarcastic, then the 25 per cent overrides the 15 per cent and I will not communicate anything other than sarcasm. The next stage is if I tell the children that God loves them and my tone agrees with my message, but in my heart I am wishing I was at home in my cosy house watching television, then who I am overrides my tone and message and again I communicate nothing. To put all this another way, we could draw on the Zulu proverb: "I can't hear what you are saying because who you are is shouting in my face."

There are three basics that we need to know. The problem is they are so basic most people overlook how important they actually are:

1. If the children don't like you they will not listen to you
We all know this to be true. When we were in school – however long ago it may have been – we learned most from the teachers we liked and the least from the teachers we didn't. It's just one of those facts of life: we learn from those we like and particularly when we think they like us. If the children don't like you, then it really is all over. They will not listen.

2. If you will not have fun with them they will not listen to you
Children will always listen to someone who has taken the time to have fun with them, to get down to their level, to play their games. Those who have taken an interest in the children's world will always have an advantage.

3. If you will not listen to them they will not listen to you
Any children's worker who has been doing the work for any significant period of time will have a story about how they were on the brink of a cliffhanger ending to their best story when a little boy or girl has shouted out, "I went to the supermarket today and I bought yoghurt."

Nothing to do with the story, but this child has waited all day long to tell the story of their adventure to the supermarket and since they didn't get the opportunity before, this seems like a great opportunity, when everyone else is quiet. We only have ourselves to blame. If at any point in the programme we had given the child a chance to talk then we could have finished our amazing story. What's worse is when the child interrupts your story with something far more serious, "My mum and dad are arguing all the time."

But the cause is the same. They were not allowed time to express themselves earlier on.

In my view these three things are basic basics. But how many people actually design their programmes to take these things into consideration? **How many people design their programmes so that children can have fun with them, so that children can talk to them, so that children can get to like them?** The answer is a lot less than 99 per cent.

If these things are important, then when the children arrive give them time to sit in a café area and eat chocolate, to play at some computers, or to bounce a ball outside with you before the teaching programme kicks off. They can share their adventures at the supermarket or their more serious concerns with life at home in the café area; they can have fun with you as they destroy you yet again on the computer games and on the basketball court, and they can just hang out with you and get to know you – and more importantly, to like you. We need some children's workers out there who are absolute heroes to their children's group. It is hard to underestimate the importance of play. The United Nations charter on the rights of the child states that children have the right to play! Play allows us opportunity to mix with the children, to learn from the children, to win the right to speak into their lives.

Having talked about preparation of the message and preparation of the messenger allow me to touch on my pet passion to end this chapter. We need to be right, we need to communicate well, but we must never lose sight of the fact that God has called us to preach, to proclaim his word. To do it with passion and integrity, with compassion and power. Ultimately, when we talk to children we are preaching a timeless message that changes lives, communities, cities and worlds. **A message which has, and will again, rock nations. Proclamation that will sometimes bypass the head and speak directly into hearts.** The need of the day is children's workers who are full of the Holy Spirit who will proclaim, in a relevant and contemporary manner, the message of the cross and the principles of God's word.

The Best Way to Communicate
The Art of the Story

The truth is, there is no better way to communicate truth than through story. Jesus knew this. Anyone watching a master storyteller at work is soon aware of it. But master storytellers are of course made, not born – unless you happen to be Welsh and then you do have an advantage!

I want to do two things in this chapter. In the latter part I'd like to look at the art of storytelling itself, but before we go there I'd like to explore a proposition: I believe that faith development itself is dependent on stories.

James Fowler, in his seminal work *Stages of Faith*,[42] writes, "children in Stage 1 combine fragments of stories and images given by their cultures into their own clusters of significant associations dealing with God and the sacred". Fowler's Stage 1 children (aged to about seven) are looking for the necessary materials to construct their understanding of God, and stories provide those materials. They need to hear stories. Without stories, they don't have the necessary building materials and they cannot build. But if we tell Bible stories then we make it possible for them to construct a healthy image of God. But even at this stage I would argue that faith development is about more than cognition (understanding) and since James Fowler's work is built on Jean Piaget's cognitive stages, it will only ever show us part of the picture. And whether Piaget and Fowler acknowledge it or not, stories are about more than cognition.

John Barton, the Old Testament theologian, writes, "Stories in the Hebrew bible do not exactly teach us duties or virtues, they engage us existentially and can deeply inform our moral life."[43] This is not only the case for Old Testament stories, but for stories in general. They have within them the capacity to engage the listener or reader on a level beyond cognition. Stories have the capacity for transcendence – a capacity to

---

42   Fowler, James, Harper and Row, 1981, p. 128.
43   Barton, John, *Ethics and the Old Testament*, London: SCM Press, 1998, p. 34.

change the listener or reader – with or without understanding.

Fowlers Stages do however give us some insight into which Bible stories we tell. He suggests that children at Faith Stage 2 (school-aged children) begin to become community aware, recognizing their own story is interwoven with the story of their community – others are involved in the story. Therefore Stage 2 becomes the place where we tell children stories of the God who comes alongside: David works well, David is helped by God to defeat Goliath, David is supported by Jonathan to outwit Saul. But Stage 2 gives us more than this. It is the first time children move away from existence defined by a series of seemingly unrelated events, to a form of existence that is understood to be a journey. Alongside this, there comes a desire to understand the journey – to bring meaning to the journey. The vast catalogue of stories stored in the previous stage is now added to, and this amalgam is the reference point from which meaning and understanding are drawn. More than simply adding to their bank of stories and drawing meaning from them, a child at Faith Stage 2 can begin to generate their own stories. So, what happens if we stock a child's imagination with stories of world missions and tell them the stories of Hudson Taylor, Gladys Aylward or Amy Carmichael at this point? I'll give you a clue. In a survey undertaken at the start of the twentieth century, a third of all those involved in overseas mission felt called to that particular country between the ages of seven and twelve – the age when their faith development had shown them there were others to reach and when they began to understand that their lives were going somewhere.

And of course, Stage 3 is generally accepted as the start of the teenage years. But some warnings of concluding that too quickly. Firstly, many of our eight-year-olds are already experiencing Stage 3 characteristics (but you knew that already right? Eight-year-old teenagers!). Children's workers have known this for a while and have been borrowing programmes from the young people's programme to try and compensate. But the next part might be a surprise. Most people (yes, that said "most") never leave Stage 3. Stage 3 has some key characteristics. It's the stage of the "significant other" – they will hero worship their leaders. It's the stage of "self-awareness" in which self-image becomes really important. And it is the age of tacit faith – "I know what I believe and I believe it strongly and I will defend it completely... I just don't know why!" It's the final point that proves particularly tricky in our world of storytelling. We need to be telling stories that are affirming, that build self-worth, that establish secure young people. There are plenty of Bible stories that will do that. But the next part is the tricky part. We need them to move to Stage 4. It should be our goal. Stage 4 is the point where they can reflect on their own practice. The point where we have taught them how to learn, not just how to receive. The dawn of spiritual maturity. But whether we like it or not (and I don't!), Stage 4 Christians have a mature faith because invariably they've gone through crisis, maybe experienced suffering, and they've come face to face with doubts having learned to build faith on it. But that's why they need stories.

Traditional sermons or, dare I say it, talks to teenagers, tend to have clean edges, conclude with everything in place and with a nice "how to..." section at the end. But the interesting, frustrating, glorious thing about life is it's messy. No clean edges, there are few situations where everything is resolved... that's why stories are so powerful, they are intrinsically messy. More often than not there are things left unresolved, there are rarely neat culminations. And that's why stories don't need endings, just stop points. Stories are incredibly potent. Transformative. And the process of moving from one *Faith Stage* to the next is one of transformation. Stories give us a theology for hard times and a theology for happy ever after. Hope and Perseverance.

But before we jump in to looking at the stories themselves, allow me the space to ask a hugely important question ... Are they sitting comfortably? This is not just an expression. Some children would love to listen to your story but can't! Allow me to explain by way of an example. Several years ago I visited a large Australian children's ministry being run out of a community centre in one of the lower socio-economic parts of the country. For the first few months of running the leaders could not get the children to listen. They were truly wild. These children didn't just write on the toilet doors they set fire to them. The change came one evening when a leader began to chat to the children and realized that many of them hadn't eaten a proper meal for several days and would probably go several more days before they got fed again. The leader realized that the children couldn't sit still because they were hungry. Using Maslow's triangle below, their physiological needs were not met, so they could not concentrate, and they certainly couldn't sit still for a story.

Some children are well fed, clothed and housed, but are deeply insecure. Again, using Maslow's, their emotional needs are not met. They need to feel secure before they can listen. It's worth thinking through the question; are your listeners sitting comfortably? What must you do to make them feel comfortable; feed them? Spend time making them feel at home? Don't take anything for granted in the twenty-first century.

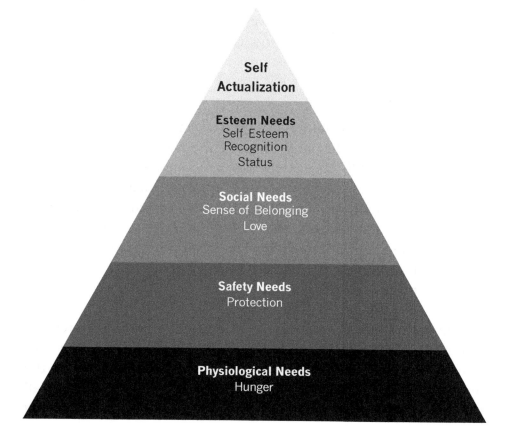

It's a journey

This is the key to the whole thing. It is a journey. Modern communicators have somehow got the idea that it is about communicating facts; about imparting nuggets of information. No. This book aims to show you how to craft an experience. It is about the joy and pain, wonder and angst, uncertainty and delight of journeying. And like any memorable journey, we are likely to be changed by it. For therein lies the crux, storytelling is transformative. At the end of the story, you are likely to be a different you to the one that entered it. Stories are transformative.

Stories move us; they operate on a level far deeper than simply cognition. And this is important because the latest research tells us that children are now exhibiting a nonlinear style of thinking – in fact, a mosaic. This is a generation that is wired for stories! The style of linear, sequential logic that has been categorized as left-brain activity is losing significance and the right-brain activities of intuition and narrative have reasserted themselves, clamouring for prominence and insisting on involvement in life and learning. Stories communicate on a whole new level.

The journey has a guide

When a story is told, rather than read, there is a whole different connection between the storyteller and the listener. Many objective studies have tested listener reactions, comparing responses to reading from a manuscript versus speaking extemporaneously, and have concluded that there is up to 36 per cent more retention in listeners and that they are instantly more sympathetic and more attentive. Bruno Bettelheim, who has undertaken extensive study on the telling of fairy tales, commented, "A story should be told rather than read. Extemporaneous speech makes the speaker seem more vulnerable and accessible and therefore more credible."[44]

Crib notes are fine, but you're only allowed a maximum of ten key statements that can be placed on an A3 sheet and taped to the floor in front of you. No more or you'll be tempted to read. Below are the ten key words to tell the story of Oscar Wilde's *The Selfish Giant* (all the stories alluded to can all be found in my 2014 book *Hanging on Every Word*):

Every day after school
Giant returns home
Nowhere to play

---

44   Bettelheim, Bruno, *The Uses of Enchantment: The Meaning and Importance of Fairy Tales*, New York: Vintage Books, 1977, p. 150.

Spring does not come
Little boy under tree
Giant plays too
Asks after boy
Older
Winter again
Little boy returns

However, Bettelheim introduces the other aspect that is so important. The credibility of the storyteller. As has already been alluded to in the previous chapter, it is the personal credibility of the storyteller that validates the story. Now, I know the stories in this book are hardly the political manifesto of a major political party approaching an election, but the same principles apply. A storyteller whose heart is not in it will mess up the delivery of the story even if she delivers every word perfectly with dazzling annunciation, razor-sharp wit, and a range of regional accents! Who we are communicates. Be a credible storyteller by ensuring that you carry yourself with integrity. Be trustworthy. I may have only told 600 primary school children the story of Gladys Aylward travelling to China this morning, but they are assessing my personal credibility as I speak and by the end they have decided whether they trust me. I did mention that this was beyond cognition, didn't I? Therefore the storyteller needs to have a heart free of baggage and a sweet spirit – not at all easy to maintain.

The journey has to start somewhere

An effective first line is the hook. Get it wrong and there is no catch, the fish swims away.

"High above the city on a tall column stood the statue of the happy prince." So starts Oscar Wilde's *Happy Prince*, and we instantly find ourselves in a different world. Looking down a huge city stretching in all directions. But you can help it further. When delivering the line I stand still and regimental like a statue, with only the slightest hint of a wobble to illustrate that I am up very high.

"It came as quite a surprise when George walked into the room and proclaimed, 'Mum, Dad... '" starts the story of George and Mr Spencer.

"The shoemaker wasn't very rich..." The opening line to Tolstoy's *Shoemaker*.

The listener is drawn into a new world. A new reality. The journey can now continue. The listener is ready to journey with you. They have been hooked.

The journey itself

Take a look around. Describe what you see. That knight riding beside you isn't just quiet, he is mocking you with stony silence. You occupy two roles. You are the artist, you are painting the scene. But you are also the servant of the story. When the story tells us that "Telemachus shouted at the top of his voice, 'This is not right'" – then the story expects a shout. And when "With his dying breath Telemachus whispers, 'This is not right'" – then that is what is expected. Use your voice. Whisper, project, pause, and then your greatest tool: be silent. Silence is our friend. Particularly with a large crowd. Any head teacher will tell you that to control a whole school assembly you do not raise your voice, you drop it.

You have the text of each of the stories, but they are alive and they can take different forms and shapes, depending on who is telling them. Here are a few more keys:

- Use precisely the right word. Say it was oval, not it was sort of round.
- Use specific, not generic words. Say pinto pony – not just horse. Say shack, mansion, lean-to, not just building.
- Use descriptive words. Say the wind whined and clawed at the corner of the house, not the wind blew hard.
- Use action verbs. Say he tore out, breezed out, strolled out – not went out.
- Use short, forceful Anglo-Saxon words. Say he died – not he passed away, next to – not contiguous.
- Use words found in your listeners' speaking vocabulary. Say swollen, not distended; I like you and not I hold you in high esteem.
- Use imitative words that imitate natural sounds. Say soothe, lull, smooth, bang.
- Use words with significant contemporary meaning. Say

home, not residence, meal not repast.
- Avoid clichés, pastoral patter, trade talk, and stale fancy phrases.

And a few more storytelling aids:

Repetition

Old tales such as "The Three Little Pigs" rely on repetition and formula with "I'll huff and I'll puff" repeated again and again. Similar systems are used when Walter asks, "You're not chicken, are you?" in the story of "Bushy and Rusty". They are there to aid in memorization. But they also build tension. A similar thing can be seen in the drip, drip, drip of Oscar Wilde's *The Happy Prince*. This leads to our next aid.

The power of three

Three drips. Two doesn't work, neither does four. Try it if you don't believe me. But also there are typically three sons in the adventure stories, there are three encounters with Farmer Brown in "Bushy and Rusty"; there are three "needs" in *The Happy Prince*; three houses in "The Three Little Pigs". There is undoubtedly a clever reason why, but sometimes it is enough just to recognize that the formula works well, so go with it.

Connect with the main characters

You need to understand the main character. Become friends with them. Know how they will respond in given situations. Understand why. They may have been written as two-dimensional characters, but you can give them life. Let them exist in the imagination of your hearers. Allow your characters to live.

The journey has to have a stop point

Old tales such as "The Three Little PigThere have been long drawn out theological debates that have run for centuries focusing on whether there are degrees of sin. I am not sure. But I can tell you the worst sin of them all. To say the words: "This means, boys and girls…

If you ever say these words at the end of one of these stories I hope they give you detention. It is the storyteller's greatest crime. **Listen!**

Great stories don't need to be explained. Oscar Wilde's *The Selfish Giant* is an incredible piece of storytelling. When I first told the story I was tempted at the end to ask the school, "Who was that little boy?" This resulted in a few answers quickly followed by the end of the assembly. A few years later, when I repeated the story, I ended with, "I can't tell you who the little boy is but maybe you'll work it out." This time there were lots more conversations and a general buzz of discovery after the assembly. But in recent years I have stopped at the end of the assembly and asked everyone to think about the story. I then say a short prayer for the school and I sit down. No explanation. No leading the children in a certain direction. No clues! The results have been staggering. Children who had no friends because they were unkind, understood from the story that kindness means friends, and it worked. Children worked out who the little boy was and why he was hurt. But one head teacher broke my heart when she phoned to say that the little boy who was struggling with the death of his granddad now knew that Jesus would look after him! That's the power of the story. To communicate to dozens of people in different ways at the same time. Stories are truly powerful. And if you have never read *The Selfish Giant* you'll have no idea what any of this paragraph means![45]

The clever chaps state it well. Bettelheim writes:

> The story communicates to the child an intuitive, subconscious understanding of his own nature and of what his future may hold if he develops his positive potentials... one must never explain to the child the meanings of fairy tales.[46]

J. R. R. Tolkien not only resisted explaining a story, he also resisted using illustrations. He commented:

> ...illustrations do little good to fairy-stories... If a story says "he climbed a hill and saw a river in the valley below," the illustrator may catch, or nearly catch, his own vision of such a scene; but every hearer of the words will have his own picture, and it will be

45   Griffiths, Mark, *Hanging on Every Word*, Oxford: Monarch Books, 2014, p. 157.
46   Bettelheim, B., *The Uses of Enchantment*, New York: Vintage Books, 1977, p. 157.

made out of all the hills and rivers and dales he has ever seen....[47]

Tolkien, the master storyteller and creator of Middle Earth, makes an interesting observation in our world of PowerPoint and DVD projectors.

The true strength of narrative comes when it is woven into the experiences and current realities of the child. When the child is allowed to learn the lessons of the story for herself, and when the morals of the story are allowed to slowly merge with her own reality and become relevant specifically to her, this is the beauty of the narrative.

The interesting, frustrating, glorious thing about life is that it's messy. No clean edges, few situations where everything is resolved; this makes a nonsense of the suggestion that all our stories must have neat endings. We simply need to take our reader to a stop point. They may well take the story further, but this allows them time to reflect on the journey so far. One of my personal favourite storytellers, Susan Howatch, uses one of her characters to talk about the creative process, below. It really does sound like the storyteller in action:

> But no matter how much the mess and distortion make you want to despair, you can't abandon the work because you're chained to it, it's absolutely woven into your soul and you know you can never rest until you've brought truth out of all the distortion, and beauty out of the mess – but it's agony, agony, agony – while simultaneously being the most wonderful and rewarding experience in the world – and that's the creative process which so few people understand.
>
> It makes an indestructible sort of fidelity, an insane sort of hope, an indescribable sort of... well, it's love, isn't it? There's no other word for it. That's the way it is. That's creation, you can't create without waste and mess and sheer undiluted slog. You can't create without pain. It's all part of the process. It's the nature of things. So in the end every major disaster, every tiny error, every wrong turning, every fragment of discarded clay, all the blood, the sweat and tears – everything has a meaning. I give it meaning. I reuse, reshape, recast all that goes wrong so that in the end nothing is wasted and nothing is without significance and nothing ceases to be precious.[48]

---

47   Tolkien, J. R. R., *Tree and Life*, Boston: Houghton Mifflin, 1965, p. 95.
48   Susan Howatch, *Absolute Truths*, Fawcett Books, 1996, p. 406.

Am I overstating all this? After all, it is just storytelling. Try it and see. I have had the privilege of telling stories in front of 5,000+ people in a single arena on a few occasions and I can assure you that there is nothing quite like that moment when thousands of people are sat in silence with mouths open hanging on your every word, desperate to know where the story will lead them. Enjoy it and see the power of stories to transform.

Stories will take you to the depths of sorrow – I have watched as the story of Gelert and the signalman's son in *A Dog Called Gelert* take a whole school to hysterical laughter and then to actual tears and then for one of the stories, back to laughter. You'll need to read them to see which does what![49]

And of course, there is one more dimension. Now that you have understood all this, maybe you can tell your own stories, new stories, stories to captivate and enthral; new stories to make us laugh and cry, new characters to enjoy. Why not?

---

49   Griffiths, Mark, *Hanging on Every Word*, Oxford: Monarch Books, 2014, p. 40.

Telling Real Bible Stories– Samuel Returned to Ramah

Ihold firmly to the assertion that teaching Bible stories to children is an incredibly powerful thing to do. Storytelling is an exceptionally powerful medium, but at the same time the intrinsic quality of truth is it always sets people free. Always. So storytelling from a book of truth is bound to be exceptionally transformational. IF we tell the real story. I'm not a fan of the polished telling of Bible stories that sterilizes the actual story and renders the characters as saint-like but inaccessible. The Bible contains the stories of real people. And we need to tell the story as it is. Below is my example taken from the story of Samuel. Not the polished cardboard cut-out story. The real story.

So let's spend a little time with Samuel. The real Samuel is my favourite Bible character – I never much liked the version of him I heard in Sunday school – or in church for that matter. Let me show you him. He is a legend. In Hebrews 11 he will be listed alongside Moses and Elijah as prophets – people who speak for God. But I suspect he is not as you had thought.

But let's go straight to his story and dive into a nice part. Jesse's house in Bethlehem. Chapter 16 of 1 Samuel – allow me to introduce Samuel the kingmaker. Jesse has been commanded to bring his sons before Samuel. And the sons pass by, Eliab comes, and Samuel is sure the Lord's anointed stands there. But the Lord speaks and says those words with which we are so familiar: "man looks on the outward appearance, but the Lord looks on the heart" (ESV). And so the sons are looked at and examined and God says, no. Don't miss that. The quote about outward appearance is helpful, but the learning is to be found in the intimacy of the relationship between God and Samuel. Samuel has conversations with God as if he were talking to a friend stood next to him. So attuned is he, he can hear the very whispers of God.

But more brothers are brought – "No", "no" and "no". And Samuel makes the necessary enquiry. Is there another son? Samuel asks the question because God has said that he must anoint one of Jesse's sons, and since he hasn't seen the right one yet there has to be another one. "Oh yes. There is." And David is brought. We'll need a whole separate article to explain why David is missed out.

So Samuel anoints David. He pours oil on him and the Spirit of the Lord comes on David. And at the end of the chapter, "Samuel returned to **Ramah**."

And of course, this is not the first king Samuel has anointed. Israel had been crying out for a king. They've never had one before and Samuel had agreed to find them a king. So 1 Samuel 9. There is a man of great standing named Kish, a Benjamite, and he has a son named Saul and on this particular day he has lost his donkeys and he is searching for them. And dusk approaches and there is a feeling that they should return home. But they hear that there is a prophet in the nearby town who might be able to help. It's Samuel. His habit was in those days to set out every year and do a tour of Israel judging disputes in each district. Today he is in the district of Zuph. The Bible tells us that the day before, the Lord had spoken to Samuel and told him that this time tomorrow a man from Benjamin would come. Anoint him to be king. And so Saul comes, and Samuel knows he's the one. He tells him, "Don't worry about the donkeys they have been found."

And he anointed Saul with oil (1 Samuel 10). And then he tells him:

- When you leave today, you will get to Rachel's tomb; two men will meet you there and tell you the donkeys have been found.
- When you leave there, at Tabor you will meet three men going to worship. They will offer you two loaves of bread, which you will accept.
- After that you will get to Gibeah and there you'll meet some prophets who will be playing musical instruments. When you encounter them the Spirit of God will come upon you and you will be changed into a different person.
- After these signs are fulfilled, go home, wait seven days and I will join you.

And that's a cool word of knowledge. I'm not that impressed by the person who stands at the front of the large conference and announces, "There's someone here with a bad back." I think they've got a chance! But Samuel's words deal with a level of detail that can only come from God. And it all happens exactly as Samuel said. Eventually Saul becomes king. And Samuel returned to **Ramah**.

But let's look at Samuel a little closer. I hate two-dimensional representations of biblical characters. There are no fairy-tale princes and princesses in the Bible and, for that matter, no fairy-tale villains. These are real people.

What's he like? Chapter 16 – those happy passages where David is anointed. The Bible records, in verse 4, that the elders of the town met Samuel at the entrance to Bethlehem and when they saw him they trembled with fear and asked, "Do you come in peace?" They trembled with fear.

In chapter 7 the Philistines invade. Samuel comes to Mizpah and offers sacrifices and prayers. And then he lifts his hands to heaven and God answers in thunder and throws the Philistines into such a panic that they run away. And then he returns to **Ramah**.

In chapter 12 Samuel makes his farewell speech. At the end of the speech he asks Israel to once again commit themselves to the Lord. They do. Then as a sign, Samuel announces: "Is it not harvest time? All is dry." And he lifts his arms and it thunders and rains. You've got this picture of this almost Gandalf-like character silhouetted by the storm.

He hears what God is whispering and he is the most powerful man in Israel. But his character is probably revealed most clearly, not when he's making kings, but when he is breaking them.

Chapter 14. The Philistines are assembling at Mikmash and Samuel is coming. He will pray and make a sacrifice and bless Israel before they advance. But he's late. And Saul panics. He decides that he can do it himself. Samuel is coming. God's timing is perfect. Wait and trust. But Saul doesn't. He makes the sacrifice himself, believing that he can do it in his own strength. And Samuel arrives…

He is not happy. "You have been foolish Saul. You didn't trust, now God will take this kingdom away from you and give it to someone with a heart like his."

And Samuel returns to **Ramah**.

Chapter 15. This is high drama. Saul is sent to fight the Amalekites. The instructions are simple. Kill them all. Even their livestock. But Saul by now is full of pride. He can do it his way. So he keeps the healthy livestock and he takes King Agag captive. But the instructions from God, through Samuel, were simple, and Samuel hears the very whispers of God. Saul kill them all. Even the livestock.

Samuel arrives. Saul says, "The Lord bless you." Samuel doesn't do pleasantries. He's never been good at small talk. He asks, "What is that sound of bleating? Why have you been so arrogant as to disobey the Lord? You have rejected God's words, so you are rejected as king."

And Samuel begins to walk away. Saul grabs Samuels robe and it tears! Oh! And Samuel declares, "In the same way, God will rip this kingdom from you, Saul."

And Saul's defence: "But I brought the livestock to sacrifice to God."

And Samuel responds, "Do you think God prefers sacrifice over obedience?" Just do what you are told Saul! And then Samuel catches sight of Agag. He tells one of the soldiers to give him a sword, and then he announces, "As your sword has made women childless, so will your mother be childless among women."

And he kills him. Very few denominations would license Samuel!

And then he returns to **Ramah**!

On a particular leadership course I attended, Samuel was presented as one of the examples. I disagreed passionately. Not to the concept of leaders who serve. That's a given. I just don't believe Samuel is a good example. You see, Samuel didn't serve anyone other than the Lord his God. And he served him passionately and zealously all his life. But he was often brutal in his passion to see God's will done.

But maybe a few more insights into Samuel's character. The people asked for a king because they didn't want Samuel's sons succeeding him. Why? Because they were godless and out of control. But what chance did he have? He was raised by Eli the priest. Eli's sons were put to death by God because, instead of behaving like priests, they stole the meat that was to be sacrificed and slept with the women. He never saw a model of how to parent.

Samuel is powerful beyond understanding; he is the kingmaker and king breaker. He hears the very whispers of God, but he is brittle, devoid of mercy, without grace, endued with a fanatical desire to serve

God and see God's will done.

And again and again we read, "And he returned to **Ramah**." In fact this phrase appears thirteen times in this one book, including the following.

David, for some time, was in the king's palace. Saul has slain his thousands but David his slain tens of thousands they cry. And Saul's jealousy is too much; he tried to kill David, but David fled to Samuel who is at **Ramah**.

Samuel dies and all Israel gathered to bury him – this is a state occasion. Samuel who judged Israel so well – God's voice to Israel has died – and the whole nation has gathered. Where have they gathered? **Ramah**.

And to understand all this, we need to go back to the start: 1 Samuel 1:1. There was a man named Elkanah. He lived in **Ramah**. He was married to a woman named Hannah and they could have no children. So once a year they travel to Shiloh and she prays. And Eli thinks she's drunk, but she's praying with such intensity. Like Rachel before her she prays, "Give me children or I die." And she promises, "Lord, if you give me a son I'll give him back to you." And Samuel is born and when he is weaned (in Jewish culture that's about aged three) he is taken and given to Eli. And God blesses Hannah with other children.

Don't miss it. He's taken from his mum when he is three years of age. He grows up with Eli in the temple. Eli who has no parenting skills. Growing up in a cold, uncomfortable temple. And the people brought sacrifice. And the Bible describes Samuel as "the child in the ephod" (1 Samuel 2:18). And we sigh and think it cute, but it's horrific. Surrounded by others making blood sacrifices and soon making blood sacrifice himself – killing animals. He should be out playing with his brothers and sisters, but he's the child priest.

Every year his mother comes with a new garment. One visit a year she brings a garment that is "too big". He will grow into it over the year. God is always putting new things on us that we must grow into. It's part of the journey. But just once a year she comes from **Ramah**.

And the Lord speaks. "Samuel." And Samuel hears, and even in this piece of narrative there is a further indictment on Eli, but Samuel, as a toddler, begins a conversation with God that will continue for all of Samuel's life.

He's not quite like the cute Sunday school lesson now is he? Samuel is so strong, so powerful. But I wonder, if he wouldn't have given the whole thing up to hug his mother and play with his brothers and sisters. And as soon as he's able, he moves back to **Ramah**. His parents would have been dead by then. But he would have been close to what could have been.

Ramah represents extraordinary sacrifice for Samuel. And not one he really had a choice in. He walks with God in a way that few people ever will, but it has cost him. Samuel is flawed, broken, fragile and brittle. As are many of the prophets. They are very, very human. Just like us.

And God looks at the heart and often finds flawed, broken, fragile humanity, and God says, "I can use that." And the cost is often great. But God continues to look for broken, fragile people who will submit to His will even through the sacrifice.

Salvation and Gifts from God

Having spent some time on communicating, we shall pause and make sure we are clear on *what* we are communicating.

Pointing a child to Christ and giving them a clear opportunity to respond to the gospel message is clearly one of the most important parts of our work with children. Allowing children to praise Jesus and to be able to hear from God themselves is a wonderful sign of their developing spiritual maturity; it is very rewarding for children's workers to see. But how do these things work in practice?

As you walk further into the chapter you will see that I do not believe that a child's relationship with God is a purely cognitive one – by which I mean it is not all down to what they understand. In many ways the notion of understanding is a red herring. I have often been faced with unhappy adults telling me that children should not be allowed to take Communion because they don't understand it. I usually ask the adult to explain to me their understanding of penal, vicarious, substitutionary atonement. When they invariably look blank I comment (gently) that it is a good job that understanding is not the gateway to Communion. As mentioned earlier, C. S. Lewis once commented (in *Mere Christianity*) that it is possible to be nourished by a meal with no real understanding of how nutrients work. I believe that God embedded eternity in the heart of the child (Ecclesiastes 3:11) and shaped and formed them in His own image (Genesis 1, Psalm 139). The child has already encountered Jesus. Our job is to help them recognize the God they have already encountered. The notion that "I led ten children to Jesus tonight" is, I'm afraid, a nonsense. Jesus was with the child long before you led them! In fact He knew them before the foundations of the earth were laid (Ephesians 1:4). That's a long time ago. In passing, this also means that the child with additional needs has no less an experience of encountering Jesus than other children. Encounter transcends cognition. If you get that, then you've grasped how incredible our God actually is.

Being a children's worker can be very encouraging, and in large groups you can usually report that at least ten children have responded to the gospel message every month. However, it usually transpires that they are the same ten children every time. Some children will raise their hands to become a Christian just because their friends do; some children will raise their hands to become a Christian simply because they know it will please you. I was at a particularly large Christian conference one year and the family we were camping near became very excited when their four-year-old son came home with a certificate saying that he had given his life to Jesus. I have no issue with these certificates. My children have many. They gave their lives to Jesus "for the first time" pretty much every year! But when I had a chat with the child who had stood to give his life to Jesus the conversation went like this:

> "That's a lovely certificate and we are all really excited for you. So why did you stand up?"
> He looked confused for a few moments then it dawned on him what I was asking. This is how he responded, "There were puppets at the front, and the boy in front of me stood up, and I couldn't see the puppet any more so I stood up too so I could see the puppet again."

Not quite the angels rejoicing in heaven situation that was being suggested.

Does that mean that children are not making genuine decisions for Christ? Not at all, in fact statistically speaking 80 per cent of the present church population made their decisions to become Christians before the age of fourteen and the vast majority of that 80 per cent made their decision before the age of twelve. So is it wrong to make appeals? Again, I don't think so. If nothing else the children's response shows that they are interested in knowing more about God. And in actuality how much more can we discern from an adult making a similar decision? One answer is that the response shows us that the person responding may want to know more. The story in the sample lesson in the Appendix is typical of the stories that I would use to invite children to respond to the gospel message. It is clear that it does not contain the whole gospel – it isn't designed to – it is designed to promote a response from those who would like to know more.

But I think there is also a wider answer that goes to the heart of the work of the Holy Spirit in transformation. C. S. Lewis captures it well in conversation between Lucy and Aslan in the *Chronicles of Narnia*. Lucy sees Aslan for the first time in *Prince Caspian* and asks Aslan if he is bigger. Aslan responds that he appears bigger because Lucy is bigger. And the more she grows, the bigger he will seem. It's a wonderful analogy particularly when most things from childhood now appear very small. It is only God who we see as bigger and more awesome the more aware we become. This idea of seeing God as bigger as we grow is of course embedded in Scripture. Luke's Gospel (2:52) records Jesus as growing in "wisdom and in stature and in favour with God and man" (ESV) (the same idea comes across in 1 Samuel 2:21b, 26 and 3:19). The Old and New Testament clearly present a child's growth in stature and in human relationship being accompanied by equivalent growth in his relationship with God.

But what has this to do with conversion? I would suggest to you an idea called "ongoing works of conversion". This is what I am suggesting. When the boy or girl is three or four and stands up on a request from their group leader or Sunday school teacher to "give their lives to Jesus", they are giving their lives to the God they have encountered and know to the extent of their knowledge and understanding. It is a genuine conversion experience. But as they grow, they find God is bigger, greater, more powerful, and so they convert again. They give their lives to how they now recognize God to be. And in later life they may convert again. On each occasion, we give our lives to God, and all are genuine conversion experiences, being transformed, moving from glory into glory. It's not far from the view the development theorists (Piaget, Fowler, Jean-Jacques Rousseau) suggest, but it is more than cognition, more than understanding. We genuinely encounter the great God of the universe on each occasion, but we perceive Him according to our ability to understand. So when we first recognize God He is the two-dimensional cardboard God, but we give our lives to Him – we convert. Later, we see Him as the three-dimensional God wanting to occupy every part of our lives. We give our lives to Him – we convert. Finally, we recognize the four-dimensional God, the one who fills all time and space, we give our lives to Him – we convert.

This is the way it should go. A singular, one-off conversion experience suggests a static, tacit faith – God is dynamic. If we take this understanding into our children's ministry we will be inviting children to give their lives to Jesus on a regular basis and they will be responding to that invitation on a regular basis.

Nevertheless, before I am accused of being all froth and no coffee, there is a cognitive element – the communication of gospel elements as John Stott used to put it. And so with the above as a given I feel the need to still follow the age-old pattern for those who are responding to an appeal to give their lives to Jesus.

Firstly, we can assume that the child's response means they may want to know more. The story in Appendix 5 is typical of the stories that I would use to invite children to respond to the gospel message. It does not contain the whole gospel – it isn't designed to. It is designed to promote a response from those who would like to know more. So what do we do when a child responds? This is a great opportunity to tell them a little more about the gospel. Allow those who have responded to meet with a leader who can more fully present the gospel elements. **Do not take the children to a different room.** Parents turning up early to collect their children will feel very uncomfortable if their child has been taken away from the main group. Talk to those who have responded in the same hall or room as the rest of the children, no matter how difficult this may prove. And once they are in the smaller group what do they need to hear about the gospel? For us to adequately explain the gospel we need to clearly understand three areas **before** we ask them for a response. God, them and Jesus.

I'll explain the theology behind these three areas, but in reality, the illustration to the right produced by Windsor-based King's Church International sums up the process of presentation. Many organizations produce booklets that communicate these gospel elements.

GOD LOVES ME: God loves us completely and unconditionally. No matter what we have done wrong, God loves us (1 John 4:16). But God is also completely holy. He is pure (1 Peter 1:16).

I HAVE SINNED: We were created good, but became **sinful**. Sin is the rubbish, the junk and garbage in our lives, the wrong things we do. Everyone has done wrong things (Romans 3:23). Someone has to pay for the wrong things we have done. It ought to be us (Romans 6:23).

JESUS DIED FOR ME: Jesus is God, who also became a person when He was born as a baby in Bethlehem (John 1:1, 14). He lived a perfect life but allowed Himself to be nailed to a cruel cross to pay for the wrong things we have done (1 Peter 2:24). He paid for the wrong things we have done by dying on the cross for us (John 3:16). All He asks is we accept His gift of forgiveness (Ephesians 2:8–9).

And after talking the children through the above (or at least a summary of the above) we can give them an opportunity to respond again:

I NEED TO LIVE 4 GOD: So we get to make a choice. To accept what He has done for us, allow Him to forgive us and choose to live for Him, or we can choose to walk away (Romans 10:13). If we ask God to forgive the wrong things we have done, He will forgive us (1 John 1:9).

At this point pray a prayer with the children that they can repeat, asking God to become their forgiver and leader. Having completed this process invite the children to promise to do two things before they go to sleep that night:

- pray the prayer asking God to become their leader and forgiver one more time in their own words
- tell someone they can trust what they have done.

What about hearing from God and spiritual gifts?

The most important element here is that children see an example of spiritual gifts in operation from adults. Whether that be in the children's gathering where the adults are the leaders or in the intergenerational gathering where all ages worship together. And in passing, I am a passionate fan of both. Every summer I stand on a platform at the start of something called New Wine, a family conference seeing some 25,000 people attend over two weeks every summer in the UK. Of that 25,000 a large proportion are children. We need 1,500 children's workers to run our children's groups. I stand on the platform and speak to the gathered children's workers, saying these words:

> If you want to see children passionately worshipping Jesus,
> then you passionately worship Jesus. If you want to see children

drawing close to God in intimacy, then you draw close to God in intimacy. If you want to see children filled with the Spirit, then you need to be. And if you want to see children move in gifts of healing and prophecy and all the rest, you need to move in spiritual gifts. It's called being a leader. You get to go first.

It works. The modelling of these things by our leaders allows children to go there too.

It is wonderful to be a children's leader when another leader has just used a spiritual gift, to simply be able to say, "That's what we call the gift of prophecy. God says that you don't have to be an adult to do that, it simply involves hearing from God and telling others what he said."

People being obedient to God is the best object lesson we will ever present.

I prefer to give the children an opportunity to share what God has been saying to them at the end of, or sometimes during, the quieter songs. Elisha in 2 Kings 3:15 asks for a musician to come so he can listen to God and proclaim His word. This is the biblical basis, but at the end of the day it boils down to style and personal preference. I have no doubt that children could listen to God and share what He is saying in total silence or, for that matter, in the middle of raucous noise. It really doesn't matter, what does matter is that children are given the opportunity to hear from God, and very often God will give them something to share with the group.

In practice, at the end of a quieter song I would explain to the children that God not only wants us to talk to him, but He also wants to talk to us. I explain that sometimes God speaks to us and what God says may just be for us. God may want to whisper in our heart that He is always with us. However, there are times when God speaks to us and the words He whispers into our hearts are for us to share with others. He may want us to tell everybody that He loves everyone, no matter what they have done. Sometimes He may show us a picture of something and tell us the meaning of the picture. Make it very clear to the children that they are in a safe environment and nobody will laugh if they get it wrong.

Some of the words that children have shared in these times have blown me away. Sometimes they have a depth and maturity that is far beyond what I would expect. Sometimes they are just very amusing. But God really does love to get involved in young lives. Children have seen maps of countries that God wants them to go to when they are older, and I've now been in this ministry long enough to see them go. Children have told other children that they don't need to be afraid any more because God will protect them and others have burst into tears as the strength of the message has hit them. Eighty per cent of our missionaries heard God calling them to the mission field as children.

I ask the children to share whatever God is telling them with another leader first before I allow them to announce it to the group. This means that we don't allow a child to embarrass themselves or for that matter share something that God is clearly and personally speaking to them about.

Some churches would call this the gift of prophecy, others would call it seeing visions. For my part, I am not particularly interested in the terminology; it is simply very exciting to see children touching God and touching the supernatural.

And of course praying for others for healing is no different. We have seen children pray for leaders and leaders healed. We have seen scars disappear – maybe that needs a bit more explanation. It was during a New Wine Festival in 2014. One of our team leaders had an intern who had been self-harming. A child prayed for him and said, "Your scars are forgiven". The intern thought that God had forgiven him for the self-harming and that made him elated. But later in the shower he saw the full extent of God's grace – the scars themselves had disappeared! Miracles happen all the time.

And having shared that last story, this final warning may seem hard, but beware too much emotion around spiritual gifts. It can be counterproductive. Children can get worked up very quickly; they can get very emotional very quickly. It is your responsibility to keep it God-centred. It's not easy, but it is important.

This short chapter is intended to overview this area. For further help, can I suggest reading David Pytches excellent book *Come Holy Spirit*[50] with an understanding that all the items listed – including the baptism in the Holy Spirit – are available to children.

---

50   Pytches, David, *Come Holy Spirit*, London: Hodder and Stoughton, 1994.

SECTION 3
A Few Misconceptions

Let's Take a Break and Barbecue Some Sacred Cows

If I were to wear spectacles with rose-coloured lenses the world would look pink; if I wore blue lenses the world would look far colder. We all wear spectacles over our minds. These spectacles are called preconceptions. We all have them. They colour the way we see things and are placed there as a result of our upbringing: our first experiences with church, our denomination, our social class.

When I first became a Christian I was put in charge of a Sunday school class and really didn't know what I was doing. After spending several weeks learning secular songs with the ten and eleven-year-old girls I was responsible for I was eventually given a "pack" of stuff from a reputable Christian supplier that contained charts and games ideas and the like. It soon became very clear to me that the group enjoyed the pop songs much more. But this "pack" was what I was supposed to teach and teach it I did, no matter how depressed everyone else in the group looked. The only representation of Christ this group were getting was dull, uninspiring and lifeless. I kept this up for many months even though the group of ten became a group of five. Someone told me that they always drop out when they get a bit older – that was over thirty years ago, and the memory still makes me cringe!

Eventually the group was reprieved and I went off to theological college for three years to learn how to do it properly. The very scary part was that the college reinforced the model I was already using – I lecture on children's ministry at many theological colleges now, so hopefully the model is slowly being eroded. Three years later I began to lead children's ministry initiatives of my own… and guess what… this is where the preconception comes in. When it came time for me to start teaching I did what I had seen. I placed one person in charge of lots of little groups split by age and gave each leader a "pack" and told them to get on with it. It was nonsense. I knew it didn't work, I knew the children didn't respond, I knew it wasn't what God was looking for, but this is all I knew – this was my preconception of children's ministry and my preconception was undoubtedly a misconception. It just didn't work.

Eventually I had to get on my knees before God and allow Him to strip the preconceptions away. Now I am always challenging what we do. Whether it be the format of local church services, the organization of the children's ministry or the way we engage with schools. I am always challenging the preconception, always asking if God has a better idea than my idea. But the analysis for me comes down to a few key questions:

- Why do we do it this way?
- Is this really working?

It keeps me fresh, but it's never easy to remove the preconceptions, especially if we've been running our programme based on them for a long time. It is probably worthwhile spending a little time here looking at some of the more familiar misconceptions I have come across over the years. I'll restrict myself to just three. You'll need to find the rest yourselves.

Misconception 1: Change the format every week

In many ways a reaction against "always doing it this way". But nonetheless, an equal and very common misconception. It is probably best explained by a short story:

> Little Jim turns up to the children's club for the first time. His mum ruffles his hair, kisses him on the cheek and tells him to have a good time and that she will be back for him later. He walks into the club discreetly wiping the kiss off his cheek. He hands in his registration form and walks into the hall. The chairs are facing the front. He chooses a seat that is empty and sits down. The songs are first and so he watches the others and then after a couple of songs he tries to join in. He doesn't know the words, but he's going to have a try. He watches the games, he listens to the announcements and then he sits through the talk time. He's enjoyed it. He hasn't actually learned anything because insecure

people don't learn. And on his first visit he is certainly insecure. At the end of the evening he leaves. His mum is waiting. She asks him how it went, he tells her it was good. She asks is he coming again? He says yes. They go home.

The following week he's back. He's not new now so he announces his name, gets it ticked off the register and boldly enters the club. Then to his horror he discovers the seats are now facing the opposite direction. He's insecure again. He's not going to learn tonight, he's insecure again – insecure people don't learn. He listens to the songs and eventually joins in: he watches the games, he hears the talk, he leaves. Mum asks him how it went, he says it was OK. She asks him if he's coming again and he says, probably. They go home.

One week later Jim is back. He walks in to discover the seats are now all gone. It's praise party night. He doesn't know what to do, where to go, where to sit. He's insecure again. He's not going to learn tonight. In fact when Mum asks him the question at the end of the night his answer is no. He's not coming back again.

Little Jim lives with Mum, his sister lives with their dad the other end of town, with his stepbrothers. Dad left last year, he's an insecure little boy. He's not unusual. Our "Change the Format Every Week" motif keeps insecure children insecure.

For some reason that I have not been able to work out we are preoccupied now with shaking people out of their comfort zones. I hear it preached a lot. But I am not sure why I need to leave my comfort zone. I like being secure, the Bible tells me that being under the shadow of God's wing is a good place to be – in a comfort zone. Things don't always go well for me. Sometimes God asks me to walk through some difficult situations and I do so from my position of being under the shadow of God's wing. You see, we don't have to leave the security of God to go off and fight our battle – He comes with us. We fight from a position of security. Secure people change things.

Let's allow our children to arrive in a warm welcoming building. Let's make it clear what they can and can't do. Let's keep the format consistent. Let them sit where they want. Don't play around with the layout all the time. Let's build secure children.

Misconception 2: Everyone Does Everything

I've seen this one on the wall of some children's clubs under the heading RULES. Let me expose this one quickly. We stand at the front and tell the children that they are all unique, special and different and behind them, under the word RULES, is this misconception. It follows the pattern that when there is a game being played everyone plays the games. Many will protest and squeal:

"We don't like playing games."

Our response comes: "In here, everyone does everything, it's a rule."

They remind you that the week before in the preaching time you made it clear that they were unique and different and special. Everyone wasn't the same. When our messages don't match our practice the Bible calls this hypocrisy!

And ultimately you become known as the club that plays games, so all the children that like playing games come to your club. All the children that hate games don't. They go to the local Baptist church where they can do crafts because they like crafts. Or to the Anglican church where they play computer games, or to the Pentecostals who have a good tuck shop. We have successfully reintroduced denominations. The games denomination, the craft denomination, the tuck shop denomination. Denominations didn't do us a lot of favours the first time around. I don't think we want to go there again.

God gave us free will enshrined in the glorious word "choice". Why do they have to go elsewhere to do the things they like? Why can't the children who like games come in and play games, and the children who like crafts come in and play crafts and those who like computer games come in and do that? And after playing computer games for a while why can't they then go and make something in crafts? And then after having all those options for an hour why can't they then sit down for teaching and praise? I can't think of any reason.

If we really believe that they are special and unique and different, then let's allow them to be special and unique and different and give them choices.

Whenever I say this in a seminar context there is usually someone who wants to tell me that allowing all the children to do what they want to do sounds like chaos. I smile and tell them that chaos comes when we try and make children do what they *don't* want to do. I have rarely had discipline issues in any of the projects I have created.

We really must ask if what we do consistently is consistent with what we teach? Let's not fall into the trap of telling the children one thing in our preaching and then having something completely contradictory in our "rules".

Allow me one more misconception in this section, the one that says:

Misconception 3: Grading is essential

This is the one that placed me in front of a group of ten and eleven-year-old girls. The group was split by age and also by gender. Curiously, it's a new idea. Well the age grading part. I think the splitting of boys and girls is several thousand years old, and Jewish!

When Robert Raikes started the very first Sunday school in 1780 it looked like this.

Mrs Critchley was in charge (I'm going to make up the rest of the names, but Mrs Critchley is named by Raikes in the documentation). She was the very first employed children's worker. And I am well informed that the salary for children's workers has changed very little since 1780. Mrs Critchley is chosen by Raikes because of her ability to communicate Jesus and her ability to keep control. That's worth pausing on. Church leaders who are looking for a new children's minister often ask me the question, "What are we looking for?" And it is the Mrs Critchley formula I always send them. You need someone who can communicate Jesus and someone who can keep control. Anything else is a bonus. But if they don't have those two things then they shouldn't employ them. Those who can keep control but can't communicate Jesus, well there's very little point, and those who can communicate Jesus but can't keep control, well, nobody is listening. We need both. Communication in a well-structured environment.

In 1780 the children's gathering would have looked like this. Mrs Critchley would be at the front ready to communicate. The hall might have several hundred children of the primary school age group (of course there would be no "primary school" at that point in history but that is the age range Mrs Critchley was dealing with). Next door there would be a room for the pre-schools (again the terminology hadn't been invented yet) primarily because every primary school aged child would bring along their younger brothers and sisters. In another room those aged twelve and thirteen would gather. The beginnings of youth ministry. No older than thirteen, because if you were fourteen you were working and regarded as an adult.

Beside Mrs Critchley would be Mrs Smith who came along to play some songs for singing time (they hadn't invented "praise and worship" terminology yet either). On the side was Mr Evans who came to ensure everyone behaved, and he was very good at it – he could control the room with a click of his fingers and a look. And at the back of the room was the wonderful administrator who could tell you who was in and who was not and the total attendance.

And that was it. Four leaders, 200 children. This was in the time when they hadn't invented terminology for "ratios" either! And that's how it ran. It ran effectively. Mrs Critchley could control hundreds, there were no issues.

In the early 1900s Jean Piaget made a pronouncement. "You can't teach a five-year-old and an eleven-year-old in the same place at the same time can you?" The Sunday schools agreed and soon a system of grading was introduced and slowly rolled out. It was to prove a disaster. By the 1950s there were not enough teachers to cater for all the groups. Bear in mind that in our Mrs Critchley scenario, only Mrs Critchley taught. The others did not sign up to teach. In the post-Piaget era, everyone had to teach. Many team members were ill-equipped to teach; many didn't like it, and – don't miss this – Mrs Critchley didn't like it either. She is gifted to teach the crowd. She doesn't want to teach a small group. This is not pride or arrogance, only a statement of gift. She likes the crowd. I have a lot of affinity with Mrs Critchley; I have never run a children's group of less than eighty, and the largest was 750. I also struggle with small groups. That's just the way it is. In the post-Piaget world, there are only small groups.

Don't miss this. For well over a century children's ministry was not graded. I go further than that. Jesus didn't grade. His intergenerational talks were such that everyone could take something from the message at their level.

In the 1950s the British Council of Churches recommended that we move the Sunday schools from the afternoon slot and embed them in the Sunday morning programme where there would be more adults available to help in the teaching. It wasn't a strategic decision, it was a way of managing the decline in teachers. But over the following decades something more subtle happened; it was almost unnoticed. In 1950 80 per cent of those attending afternoon Sunday school were from unchurched homes. By 1980, when the move to Sunday mornings was almost complete, only 20 per cent of the Sunday morning attendees were from unchurched homes. And by the year 2000 the number attending morning worship from unchurched homes was less than 1 per cent.

It's a knee-jerk reaction in the 1900s. The response to the question, "How can a five-year-old and an eleven-year-old learn maths in the same class at the same time?" should have been responded to thoughtfully. The correct response, of course, is when we start teaching maths in our children's groups then we will grade, but as it is, what we do has more in common with the school assembly (collective worship as part of the school day) than it does the lessons that fan off from it. And the majority of school assemblies I conduct have five- to eleven-year-olds together in the same place at the same time. We don't teach mathematics or English literature, we proclaim the gospel. The timeless gospel that Jesus proclaimed. The gospel that young and old came to listen to together, the one where grandparents and grandchildren sat side by side to hear and each understood on their own level. *The timeless gospel which sometimes bypasses the brain and hits the heart.* The glorious gospel which transforms young and old, which confuses the Pharisee but leaves the young boy saying, "I have these fish and loaves, will they help?"

It is also worth pointing out that we should always have a long-term view of children's ministry. The five-year-old may not "get it" today, but we are expecting to present the same lesson to them in four years' time. If we combine our groups, then we allow the whole range of God-given gifts to function. Here are some examples of the gifts that can be released into children's ministry if we change the paradigm:

Pastors

Obviously the word most closely associated with this would be shepherding. To care for the flock. When Jesus talks to Peter at the end of Matthew's Gospel he extols him to "take care of my sheep". This is what we are looking for within this gift: someone who can take care of God's lambs. Someone with an affinity for getting alongside those who are hurting, or needy or simply those who need to feel loved. We are all called to pastor, but there are people who excel in this area. They may not be the best teachers or leaders, their administration skills may be non-existent, but their ability to care sets them apart as people we desperately need within the context of children's ministry.

Administrators

Not just those who can count the money from the tuck shop, but those with a clear God-given ability to organize. To ensure that everything is set up on time, that the registers are correct, and the rent is paid. As you will see under the chapter on infrastructure (The Children's Club, "The People", p. 217), these people are as important to the growth and development of your work as are the evangelists.

Evangelists

Which leads us nicely to the evangelists. Those with an ability to make the gospel bite-sized and easily digestible. Those with an ability to reap the harvest and to inspire and equip others to do the same. Part of my gifting lies here – I can fill buildings with children by accident when others spend months trying to achieve the same thing by design. It's an area of gifting, but a caution is necessary: evangelists can fill your club, but if you only have evangelists they will also empty it again. They may refill it shortly afterwards, but it will be with a completely different group. They need to be surrounded by lots of other gifting.

Hospitality

When our project used to run on Saturday the leaders would arrive a couple of hours early to eat breakfast together and pray together before the club began. It was not my idea. Someone with the gift of hospitality said they would like to do it for us – nobody objected. People with this gift facilitate the building of teams. They may never want to be directly involved in teaching the children, but that doesn't mean they can't use their gift within the children's clubs or to welcome the children as they arrive.

Apostles

Don't get put off by the word. Apostle is simply another gift. It is not more special than the others. Apostles are those with an affinity for making Jesus known in places where Jesus is not known. They have an ability to build. They can be incredibly visionary and see what needs to happen to fulfil the vision. They can develop new projects, they can proclaim the gospel, they can administrate, but they still need the support of others.

> "The harvest is plentiful but the workers are few. Ask the Lord of the harvest, therefore, to send out workers into his harvest field" (Luke 10:2, NIV)

So we pray:

> Heavenly Father, we pray for the workers with the right gifts – for teachers and pastors, for administrators and those with gifts of administration and with wisdom, for those with faith and those with the gift of help and service. We pray that we'll use each person in the area of their gifting, for them to grow and feel fulfilled by the role they fill and as a role model for the children. **Amen.**

SECTION 4
Practical Help

Safeguarding — Lisa Macbeth

The safety of our children when involved in our activities is clearly a priority. Lisa Macbeth is the onsite Safeguarding Officer for the New Wine Festivals that see 25,000 on site every summer. She shares some of her wisdom in this vital area with us below.

Whether you are brand new to children's ministry or have been involved for years, it is important to be up to date and "refreshed" when it comes to safeguarding matters and child protection. It's important because, as ministers of "good news" you want to do the very best by the children and young people you come into contact with, and you never know what situation you might find yourself in or what might be disclosed to you. Knowing the best ways to respond is crucial if you are going to be a good minister of the gospel. You may think that safeguarding is just about long, wordy policies that tie people up in knots, and a comprehensive policy covering children, young people and vulnerable adults is important, but it's not everything. You may think it's about DBS forms and the hassle that needs to be gone through to get checked every few years, and these checks are essential in recruiting suitable workers but, again, that's not it. Maybe you think about child protection and your mind immediately goes to the worst cases of abuse that are shown on the news and in the papers.

Child protection is about keeping children, young people and vulnerable adults safe; it's about protecting them and helping them to protect themselves, and it's about helping them if they are in unsafe and abusive situations. Child protection is also about responding to any concerns you have in the right way and it's about covering you as a worker by you knowing best practice in your work.

You

Because you are older than the children you are ministering among, because your groups and activities are exciting places to be, because parents are reliant on you for the care of their children, you are in a position of trust; a responsible and privileged position to hold. You are a role model to the children you work with, in the formal times when you're "working" but also when you're in contact with them in other situations, or when you bump into each other. Children will look up to you as their leader and want to copy what you do out of respect and admiration for you. You may be a carer for children, especially some of the youngest and most vulnerable ones in your groups. You are a mentor to children, and their teacher; you help them develop their knowledge and skills, their behaviour and their relationship with God. You are in the honoured position of being their enabler, helping them to encounter the living God and ushering them into His presence. A responsible and privileged position to be in.

And don't forget that child protection doesn't just cover the children in your groups and activities, but also your young team members aged seventeen and under, so good practice applies to all those under eighteen.

Discipline

Discipline isn't simply about telling children off when they've been "naughty". Discipline is providing appropriate boundaries that mean children are safe and able to get the most out of the activities on offer. Discipline is encouraging and building children up and therefore it should be something positive. But, sometimes, children stretch the boundaries and break the rules. This might be for a whole host of reasons: they're bored, they're angry or upset about something, they're worried and don't know how to express it, they want to fit in with their friends and peers. When this happens you need to help children to get back inside the boundaries so you discipline, always out of a place of love and never anger. It is never appropriate to smack or hit or be violent towards a child in your care. Don't shout at them either – it isn't respectful and it doesn't work anyway. Shouting can just escalate a situation. If you feel yourself getting angry in a situation, remove yourself and ask someone else to take over so that the problem is handled well and the child treated with dignity and respect at all times.

Be quick to praise and encourage children, especially the ones who are quieter or always well behaved. Children sometimes act up and misbehave because they want your attention and if that's always going to the children who are messing around, the good ones may join in too. Children may also push the boundaries if they are bored, so don't let them become so. Help them engage with an activity that's on offer. If nothing gets their interest, maybe review what's on offer. Children have an innate sense of justice and fairness so be consistent and fair in how you treat all children. Some might need additional support or attention because they have additional needs; children can be helped to understand this, but generally children can get angry and upset if they feel as if they are being treated differently or unfairly compared to someone else. Overall, it is crucial to treat all children, regardless of their behaviour, with respect and dignity. They bear the image of God and therefore are of infinite value and worth and deserve to be treated in ways that honour this.

Appropriate touch

For a long while, workers with children and young people were nervous and perhaps even scared to have any physical contact with children as they were unsure as to whether this was appropriate or not. Physical contact with children is perfectly acceptable, even necessary, provided it is done in ways which are appropriate. Children need to be touched; they may need help with washing their hands, the youngest ones may need a nappy changed, a hug when a child is upset is comforting and you may need to administer first aid. You may also have the honour of praying for children and laying hands on them as you pray. So what is appropriate touch? Firstly, it needs to be public. A hug in a public place, in the context of a wider group is very different to one which is in a dark corner, or away from others or hidden. When physical contact isn't public, you as a worker are much more vulnerable as you are open to misunderstanding and accusations. As well as being public, appropriate touch needs to be child-initiated. It needs to be about their needs and what is for their very best. If it is about your needs or making yourself feel good in some way, then it is inappropriate and you need to step away. And appropriate touch needs to be godly; it needs to honour at all times the child that is bearing the image of God. Ask yourself, especially when laying on hands in healing prayer, if it is an appropriate place to touch a child or young person and if you are in any doubt, I am confident that God can work via the shoulder! Appropriate touch: public, child-initiated and godly.

Abuse

The prayer that should be prayed with regard to handling concerns or disclosure of abuse is for the wisdom to not trivialize or exaggerate the issues. You don't want to squash it and make it smaller than it is but, similarly, you don't want to make it a bigger deal than it is and blow it out of proportion. There will, sadly, at one time or another, be children in your groups or activities who have or are experiencing abuse and part of being in a position of trust is being able to recognize the signs and symptoms of it and knowing how to respond.

Abuse of children is categorized into four areas: physical, emotional, sexual and neglect. Physical abuse is anything that is violent and physically harming, and includes hitting, shaking and burning for example. The signs of physical abuse are strange and unexplained injuries and marks on the body but also behaviour such as jumping at sudden movements because the child expects violence to be shown towards them. Emotional abuse is anything that has an adverse effect on a child's emotional wellbeing and development. This could be being told that they are unloved or worthless, or someone putting inappropriate expectations on a child according to their age and stage of development. Bullying is emotional abuse. Spiritual abuse is also included here. Signs of emotional abuse are children being withdrawn and extremely lacking in confidence, but also the opposite and their inappropriately seeking your attention and love.

Sexual abuse is forcing a child into sexual activity, whether they know it or not. Signs of this are physical marks on the body, a child with sexual knowledge beyond their years or sexualized behaviour. Forcing a child into watching sexual activity is also abuse even though there is no contact. There would in these situations be no physical marks to observe but possibly some of the other behavioural signs. Neglect is when a child's basic needs for food, clothing, shelter, are routinely not met. Signs of this are extreme malnourishment, the child being exceptionally smelly and dirty, the child excessively eating or stealing food. They may also lack in all areas of development. Please don't panic. Not every report of smacking or argument at home is abusive. But some children will be in unhappy, unhealthy, abusive situations.

So, abuse presents itself in different ways: an injury or marks on the body; behaviour that is over-sexualized; jumping at sudden movements; extreme lack of self-esteem; presentation – a child who is malnourished or exceptionally smelly and dirty. Abuse may also be disclosed to you directly or through clues or hints in a conversation. A disclosure may be about a current abusive situation happening to them, it may be about something that is happening to someone else or it may be a disclosure of something that has happened in the past. All three types of disclosure need to be recorded and reported to the appropriate person in your organization. Spotting the signs of abuse can be a bit like doing a jigsaw puzzle. One little incident or bruise is noted but nothing more. But if further concerns are raised about a child, putting them together builds up a bigger and more complete picture which may need to be handled in a more official and significant way. Ensure that you know your organization's safeguarding officer and that you know how to report minor and significant concerns when you have them.

If a child or young person discloses something to you the best thing that you can do is to listen. If a child has chosen you to speak to it is because they trust you and they trust you to do the best for them. Abuse takes away power and by hearing a child's disclosure you are now in a power relationship with them. By listening to them you are giving them back their power which can be an important moment for the child. Be accepting and calm and show this by smiling and nodding. Inside, your heart might be pounding and your mind running at a hundred miles an hour as you work out what you need to do, but on the outside you need to appear calm and accepting. Don't promise confidentiality as you are not going to be able to keep this to yourself. You can reassure the child that you are not going to shout it from the rooftops, or tell their friends, or get them in trouble but that you are just going to tell the person or people that can help them get into a happier and healthy situation. You will do your best for them. Also reassure them that they have done the right thing in talking to you. Once the conversation has finished you need to follow your organization's procedure in terms of recording and reporting what was said to you. It is important to record the key pieces of information as soon as you are able to. Don't make notes as the child is talking to you but if you can recall some of the exact words or phrases used, it may be useful later on. Don't hang around before reporting what has happened and remember that wisdom is needed to not trivialize or exaggerate what has been disclosed to you.

Prayer ministry

One of the privileges of being a minister of the gospel is praying with children so that they encounter the living God. While you might think about how you go about that in your context, there are some safeguarding principles that are important however you are involved in prayer ministry. When you pray, be supervised. Work in pairs and in the context of a larger team and group. This protects you as a worker. Don't pray just one-on-one and don't do it away or hidden from the main group or activity. Ask the child if you can pray for them and explain what you're going to do. The child doesn't have to be prayed for, they have a choice so respect it if they say no thanks. Ask before laying hands on and think about appropriate touch. Remember that God can work via the shoulder! Pray encouraging prayers. God is a good, good God who loves His children endlessly and He has good things for them and good things to say to them. You can therefore pray the good, positive and encouraging prayers over children with confidence. Because prayer ministry is about children encountering God, encourage them to pray with lots of different people rather than just you. If you're the one that prays with them each time, ministry can become about you and the child rather than them and God.

A few basic principles

You shouldn't find yourself on your own with a child or group of children. Try to always work in pairs and the context of your larger teams and groups. Don't arrange to meet up with children or young people outside the group because this especially makes you vulnerable as a worker to misunderstanding and accusation. If you do bump into children from your activities round and about say hi and have a chat but don't get caught into much more than that. And remember that you are a role model, off-duty as well as on. Particularly among your team and younger team members, maintain good relationship boundaries, again, hanging out in groups rather than couples. Your buildings and spaces for children's ministry need to be safe and secure places so have a way of identifying who is working with the children so that anyone who isn't part of the team is recognizable and can be challenged if need be. Have good recruiting procedures with regard to safeguarding; take up references and ensure DBS checks happen. Also ensure you have appropriate procedures in place for those in and around your organization who shouldn't be working with or having contact with children.

A parting word

Each child and young person is of infinite value to God. In all that you do, be committed to always expressing this value. Work at keeping the children in your care safe from harm and to always doing your best to help them enjoy the groups and activities you offer. In this way you are modelling and extending God's Kingdom.

The Beginner's Guide

The aim of this chapter is to show you how to start a children's club from scratch. It will give you a timescale for activities and, in some cases, expected outcomes. The difficulty with presenting practice is it doesn't always translate into every situation. Hopefully the preceding chapters will have built in enough principles to allow the discussion of practice. But again the warning, this section is meant to help, not to hinder; it is here as your slave and not your master. Use it, but don't be confined by it.

There are many issues that need to be weighed before you start an outreach children's club, since once something is up and running it is very hard to change its form or shape. It has always been my preference to start from scratch, as taking over from someone else is always going to be difficult. But I am aware that this is not always a possibility and some diplomacy skills may be needed to reform an existing club. But don't believe the lie that you must wait until all the conditions are right, until you have the right staff, until you are all experts at the programme, until you have all the equipment you need. If you wait for all these things, you will never start. Most things can be corrected en route. Just start. It'll never be the perfect time, but **God blesses people on the journey. Not while they're waiting for the perfect travelling conditions.**

The Timetable for the First Two Years

The WHY section is simply a reminder of what has been mentioned in the previous chapters. For a full explanation of WHY, refer to the appropriate chapter.

WHEN	WHAT	WHY
Pre-start	Take some time to pray and understand the area you are working in. If you are new to the area this is particularly important.	God may have a specific key that will enable you to establish the whole thing so much more quickly. Give God time to speak to you.
January to July (Year 1)	Make contact with one or more schools and schedule some assemblies.	Schools will be the place the children who attend your club will come from.
January	Begin to share your vision and form your team.	Your ability to reproduce leaders will be the single most important factor that determines the extent of your vision.

February	Begin to think finance. Are there local grant organizations that can help with start-up funding. Are there opportunities for child-based businesses? Can you start an after-school project in your building? How about a holiday play scheme in the summer?	Vision will always need provision.
April	Send the schools letters advertising assemblies for June and July.	
August	If you have children already linked in take them to summer camp.	Summer camp is an excellent opportunity to have significant input into your children's lives. It gives you six days away with them.
	Run your holiday play schemes.	A chance to bring in some extra income, but also an opportunity for spiritual input over a week.
September	Start your business opportunity or activate your other sources of income.	
	Begin to advertise your children's club in schools, in shop windows, on social media, by word of mouth.	People will not come if they don't know it exists.
	Staff training night. To complement all the informal training nights up until now.	Invest in your team. Give regular training and input.

October	Launch your children's club.	The rubber hits the road! Time to put it all together.
November	Hold a community event, for example a parents' party.	This never was, and never will be, just about reaching children. This is about winning families.
December	Christmas special for all the children you now have contact with. Make it a big one with selection boxes for all those who attend.	The big end-of-year bash will close your first year in style. Make sure **all** your child contacts are invited – schools, holiday play schemes, children's club.
	Send school letters out for January, February and March assemblies.	Get all your school assembly administration out of the way quickly.
	Send Christmas cards to all your contacts.	It's *always* about relationship.
	Staff/leaders' party.	Work hard but also play hard. Reward your leaders. If at all possible have a great night together and don't allow them to pay!

January (Year 2)	Restart children's club.	
	Start small groups.	Purposeful discipleship happens best in small groups.
April	Easter special for all the children you know.	
	If you are starting a church from children using the children's work as your start point, then start a Sunday service now. Make Easter Sunday your first service.	
	If no church plant then run a community event here – a swimming night, maybe, or a family fun day.	
	Don't do any children's activities or schools work in April; evaluate here.	Don't move into headless chicken mode. Keep sharp and focused. You achieve this by stopping and evaluating from time to time.
	Send the schools letter advertising assemblies for June and July.	
May	Restart the children's club.	

July	Community event – barbecue with entertainer.	
August	If you have children already linked in take them to summer camp.	
	Run your holiday play schemes.	
September	Begin to advertise your children's club in schools, in shop windows, on social media, by word of mouth.	
	If you started from scratch then start your youth activities now. If you didn't then ensure your children are making a smooth transition into the youth department.	Children don't stay children for long. They will need to move into a dynamic youth programme eventually.
	Staff training night. To complement all the informal training nights up until now.	
	Send schools letters to advertise assemblies for October to December.	
October	Launch your children's club.	
November	Hold a community event – parents' party.	

December	Christmas special for all the children you now have contact with. Make it a big one with selection boxes for all those who attend.	
	Send Christmas cards to all your contacts.	
	Advertise your Christmas services to all your contacts especially Christingle and Carols by Candlelight.	
	Send schools letters out for January, February and March assemblies.	
	Staff/leaders' party.	

Timetable for a Normal Year

January	Start children's club. Start small groups for purposeful discipleship.
April	Easter Special for all the children you know. Community event here – swimming night maybe. Send the schools letter advertising assemblies for June and July.
May	Restart the children's club.
July	Community event – barbecue with entertainer.
August	If you have children already linked in take them to summer camp.
	Run your holiday play schemes.
September	Begin to advertise your children's club in schools, in shop windows, etc. Ensure all your children who are eligible are incorporated into youth group. Staff training night. Send schools letters to advertise assemblies for October to December.
October	Launch your children's club.
November	Hold a community event – parents' party possibly.
December	Christmas Special for all the children you now have contact with. Send Christmas cards to all your contacts. Advertise your Christmas Services to all your contacts. Send schools letters out for January, February and March assemblies. Staff/leaders' party.

Timetable for the Southern Hemisphere
—by Alison Champness

The WHY section is simply a reminder of what has been mentioned in the previous chapters. For a full explanation of WHY refer to the appropriate chapter.

WHEN	WHAT	WHY
Pre-start	Take some time to pray and understand the area you are working in. If you are new to the area this is particularly important.	God may have a specific key that will enable you to establish the whole thing so much more quickly. Give God time to speak to you.
July – November (Year 1)	If teaching Scripture is allowed in primary schools in your area, make contact with the Scripture coordinator and ask if you can teach a class (or two) in the school/s that are closest to your church. Ask if they are doing Christmas or Easter assemblies and join the team! If Scripture is not allowed to be taught in your area, ask your closest school if you can volunteer to help them with a programmes such as reading or breakfast club (you can also do this in addition to teaching Scripture to build some good relationships). You may also like to join the P&C (Parents and Citizens' Association – or equivalent) to become part of the school community.	Schools will be the place the children who attend your club will come from. Developing a good relationship with the school is very important. If you build trust with the school, after a while they may allow you to advertise your children's club/ events in their newsletter.

	Begin to share your vision and form your team. Meet with people individually and/or together. Ask each person to fill in a form giving contact details, area/s where they would like to help and their WWCC or WWVP number (Working With Children Check/Working with Vulnerable People) or give them details of how to get one.	Your ability to reproduce leaders will be the single most important factor that determines the extent of your vision.
September	Begin to think finance. Are there local grant organizations that can help with start-up funding? Are there opportunities for child-based businesses? Can you start an after-school project in your building? Can you share the vision with your congregation and ask for donations to help get your new ministry started?	Vision will always need provision.
31 October	Run a "light party" in your church/hall/grounds for families as an alternative to Halloween. Have bouncy castles, face painting, sausage sizzles, games, etc. Ask to advertise in local school newsletters and radio stations as a safe, fun alternative to Halloween.	This is not just about reaching children – it's about connecting with families.
November	Liaise with the Scripture coordinator to email the schools asking permission to do Christmas assemblies and confirm date/s and hall usage.	
December (early)	Christmas assemblies in schools.	Finish with schools early in December as they are busy with end-of-school year activities.
	Family Christmas carol service or crib service.	Invite the community and have some fun – be creative!
January	Have a good rest and enjoy Christmas holidays!	
February (early)	Engage with your funding opportunities or activate your sources of income.	
	Advertise your children's club in schools, in shop windows, on social media, by word of mouth, and so on.	People will not come if they don't know it exists.
	Staff training night. To complement the informal meetings you have had up until now.	Invest in your team. Give regular training and input.

Mid – late Feb	Launch your children's club.	The rubber hits the road! Time to put it all together.
March	Liaise with the Scripture coordinator to ask the schools for permission to do Easter assemblies and confirm date/s and hall usage.	
April	Run an Easter holiday club and invite children from your programme/s and new children from local schools. (If the school holidays have Easter in the middle – the week leading up to Easter is a great time to have a holiday club as the teaching can be very focused on the Easter/gospel message.)	Engage your high school youth to help as small group leaders, for drama, music, games, etc.
May	Start-up children's club for Term 2. Invite new children from holiday club to children's club.	
July	Use the July school holidays to rest, re-evaluate and plan for the next term.	
July (end)	Restart the children's club.	
	If you don't already have a youth group (high school age) begin to plan to start one in Term 4 (after October school holidays).	
September	Announce that children in Year 6 can also start attending the youth programme in Term 4 (after October school holidays).	
October (Term 4)	Re-start children's club in Term 4. Ensure the Year 6 children are making a smooth transition into the youth department.	Children don't stay children for long. They will need to move into a dynamic youth programme to continue being discipled.
31 October	Light party for families of the community.	
November	Liaise with the Scripture coordinator (and schools) re Christmas assemblies.	

December	Christmas special for all the children you now have contact with. Make it a big one to celebrate Jesus as the reason for the season.	
	Advertise your Christmas services to all your contacts.	
	Staff/leaders' party.	Work hard but also play hard. Reward your leaders. If at all possible have a great night together and don't allow them to pay!

Timetable for a Normal Year (Southern Hemisphere)

January	Have a good rest and enjoy summer holidays!
February (early)	Begin to advertise your children's club in schools, in shop windows, etc.
February	Start the kid's club.
March	Contact primary schools about Easter assemblies.
April	Easter assemblies.
Term 1 (end)	Easter holiday club.
April/May	Invite children from holiday club to kids' club.
July	Use the July school holidays to rest, re-evaluate and plan.
October (Term 4)	Ensure the Year 6 children are incorporated into youth group.
31 October	Light party for families of the community.
November	Liaise with schools re Christmas assemblies.
December	Christmas assemblies (early Dec).
	Christmas special for all the children you now have contact with.
	Advertise your Christmas services to all your contacts.
	Staff/leaders' party.

The Children's Club

The People

Registration

Three members. This is where you meet the parents. This is the initial contact point. First impressions do last, so put some of your best in here. The registration people will also need to be armed with information regarding trips, etc. This is the place to base your administrators.

Welcome person

An adult, or several adults, who greet the children on arrival and give a quick guided tour and breakdown of the format to those who are new. This is the place to base your pastors.

Activity supervisor

Each activity such as a bouncy castle, computers, etc, needs to be supervised by an activity supervisor. This can be one of your teenagers as long as they are prepared to be responsible.

Technical

A person who operates the PA, DVDs, projector, etc., is invaluable. If done well this will help you greatly; if done badly this can destroy your programme.

Front people

A front person with the possible addition of a second for illustrations. If you work with two front people who know what they are doing and have obvious communication gifts, then introduce a third who can develop and learn. As they come to maturity in this gift then release more to them. This is a continual process and will allow you to move or sow out into other children's work. The choice of the third person is very important. They may not be the most gifted at first, but they must be humble, teachable and have the heart of a servant. Don't choose anyone without these qualifications. The front is the place for your evangelists and teachers and maybe your apostles.

Small group leaders

For most of the programme these people float around checking everyone is OK. Talking to children, sitting in the café area with them, relaxing with them, getting to know them, caring for them. The people with pastoral gifts and a heart for children thrive in this position. But they come into their own during ministry times when they gather their small group for feedback and prayer.

Others

If you run crafts as part of your programme then you will need artistic people. A qualified first aider should not be overlooked. Members of the team will also need to be involved in the weekly visitation programme. You may also have a person to be the team leader of each team. Our green team leader is presently Gregory the Green!

During the programme part of the evening there will need to be a sprinkling of leaders in each team. Problems should not be dealt with from the front but sorted quickly from within the team. For the staff, as well as for the children, it will be a process of education.

The Programme

PROGRAMME	
Section 1	Welcome
	Rules
	Prayer
	Introductory praise
	Game 1
	Praise
	Fun item 1
	Game 2
	Fun item 2
	Bible text
	Announcements
	Interview
	Worship time
Section 2	Bible lesson
Preaching	Illustration 1
Time	Illustration 2
	Illustration 3
	Story
	Prayer/ministry

Free play (30 minutes)

Listen to some basic truths. If you will not have fun with them, they will not listen to you; if they do not like you, they will not listen to you. If you will not listen to them, they will not listen to you. Spend the first thirty minutes playing with them. Having fun. Listening to the stories of their week.

Welcome (3 minutes)

This is a chance to welcome the children, but also an opportunity to have fun with them. I prefer to lead the programme with others at the front; for example, the score person, team leaders, your trainee leader. This allows comical banter between the two.

Rules (2 minutes)

If there are no clear rules then the children have no discipline guidelines. Children won't know what is or isn't acceptable in the context of this gathering. Only two simple rules are necessary:

- Nobody leaves their seat. If they need to go to the toilet then they must put their hand up and ask permission from a leader to go.
- When you ask for quiet, everyone sits down, focuses on the front and makes no sound.

These two simple rules will keep everything controlled. Children feel safer and more secure in a disciplined atmosphere. There must be a method of enforcing the rules. We use the following twofold system:

Positive reinforcement: If a team is particularly good – they sit well, they listen well, they cheer the loudest, they win a game – then they get to roll the dice. The score from the dice is added to their overall score. The team with the most points at the end of the term get the biggest prizes; the other teams also receive prizes, but lesser prizes; for example, at the end of the Easter term the winning team will receive an Easter egg; the other teams a cream egg.

Negative reinforcement: If a child talks after the whistle has gone or is not sitting and facing the front then they instantly lose six points from their score.

> TIP: You don't have to bring prizes every week. Keep a running score for each team and inform them that they are working towards the highest score at the end of term. The team that comes first will receive the largest selection box/Easter egg, and the other two teams will receive small selection boxes/ Easter eggs. Also, the age-old tactic of rewarding those who attend the most, with attendance prizes being given out at the end of term, will ensure that you don't hit the spasmodic attendance common to many children's clubs up and down the country.

Prayer (5 minutes)

In two sections:
- **Giving thanks:** Children who have prayed for something the week before (or several weeks before) and whose prayers have been answered should be asked to come and tell the others how God answered their prayer.
- **Bringing needs:** Some of the children will want to pray for certain things. Allow them to come and mention what they are praying for and ask God together to answer prayer.

Remember, when children have prayers answered they need to be invited to the front to give God thanks.

Longer prayer nights (15 minutes)

Some nights you may wish to hold an extra-long prayer section. You can do this in several ways:

P.R.A.Y.

The four corners of the building are given the letters P, R, A and Y respectively. If there are more than forty children then the centres will also need to be used as follows:

A leader is placed at each base and the children are split into four groups (eight for above). The children start at one of the bases, but will only remain there for two minutes each. After two minutes they will move clockwise to the next base. The bases are:

P FOR PRAISE

In this base the children will stand in a circle and give thanks for one thing which is good in their lives. "God thank you for my family," "God thank you for the children's club," "God thank you that I'm healthy." If they visit another P base then the leader may simply talk them through all the things we have to be thankful for: salvation, creation, life, eternal life.

R IS FOR REPENT

In this base the children will be reminded by the base leader that all of us have done things wrong, things that hurt God. This would be a good time to quietly think about things we have done wrong that hurt God and maybe ask God to forgive us.

A IS FOR ASK

At this base one or two children might lead in prayer and ask God for a good night, or maybe a safe journey home at the end. Or maybe there are specific requests for parents who are sick.

Y IS FOR YOURSELF

In this base the children will be encouraged to ask God for something for themselves. Give them quick guidance on what sort of things, but allow the children to ask God to bless them, or to give them a good night at children's club.

From time to time children will spend their Ask and their Yourself time asking God to let their team win. Don't be worried by this; I'm not sure if God has ever got involved in the scoring system at children's club.

Walk

Send the children to walk around the building on the outside. Send a leader first and then after they have travelled five metres send the first child. His instructions are simple:

- He is going to walk and talk to God in the same way that he might walk and talk to a friend; he is going to tell God how he feels and what is bothering him, etc.
- He is never going to lose sight of the person in front.
- He is never going to catch up with the person in front; there will always be a five-metre gap.

When the child has gone five metres send the next until all the children have gone. This calls for close supervision and we need to send adults in between every five or six children.

Circles

- Ask the children to find a space. In the space ask them to talk to God about themselves for one minute.
- After one minute the children join together with another child and together they pray for each other. They put their hands on each other's shoulders and in turn pray something like: "God help my friend learn more about you."
- After one minute the two join with another two and pray in their four that God will give them a good night.
- After one minute the four join with another four and pray that God will look after their families – or something similar.
- After one minute the eight join with another eight and pray that God will...
- And so it continues until you have one very large group. You then pray for the whole group.

Praise (7 minutes)

Some lively songs. There are two slots for praise. Make sure you use the first slot for songs they know which contain lots of actions. New songs can be introduced in the second section. Some of the children may not enjoy singing – make it worth six points for best team singing; suddenly you'll find they enjoy it a lot more.

Game 1 (5 minutes)

Games differ from week to week. But the following points are important:

- In order to play a game they must answer a question on last week's lesson.
- Choose one person from each team and then allow that person to choose the rest of the team.
- Give points for the teams that cheer people the loudest.
- Play music while the game runs. Fast music. Live music if possible. If not, CDs.
- The first team to complete the game must sit down.

Praise (10 minutes)

The second praise slot allows for a longer praise session with several songs being used together. Encourage banners, streamers, dancing, etc. Allow some of the children to form a praise group that stand with a microphone to lead the others. I have included a list of good songs and musicians for children in the Recommended Resource section (Appendix 7).

Fun Item 1 (5 minutes)

We use several fun items to enhance the programme. Be creative with your ideas.

Guess the Leader

We use this slot to play a game called "Guess the Leader". We reveal an interesting fact regarding one of the leaders, or one of the children. For example, "This leader used to live in Spain." Then four leaders are chosen who all try and convince the children that they used to live in Spain. The children then have to "guess the leader" who really was telling the truth. A variation on this theme is to show a picture of the leader as a baby and the leaders all have to try and convince the children that they are the person in the picture.

COMMENT: My favourite "guess the leader" is the leader who was at the theatre. In the interval she went to the bathroom, and on her return she sat in her seat and leaned over to kiss her fiancé's neck – the children never fail to go "ughhh!" at this point. The "fiancé" then turned round and his wife leaned over and gave this particular leader a very annoyed look. The leader had sat in the wrong seat and kissed the wrong person. You'd be amazed at what your leaders have done, and also how keen their friends are to tell the stories!

Strip search

Here is an idea from an old Saturday morning television programme that helps with getting to know the children or leaders. Play some background music and then for one minute ask the leader questions about their preferences, under the three categories:
  • Awake or asleep
  • Music or reading
  • Chocolate or fruit

Here are some sample questions to be used:
  • Sweets or chocolate?
  • Shoes or trainers?
  • Bath or shower?
  • MacDonald's or Burger King?
  • Cap or hat?
  • Dogs or cats?
  • Spring or autumn?
  • Pepsi or Coke?
  • Cinema or DVD?

Buy it or bin it

A chance for music and DVDs reviews. It gives the children a chance to bring in the DVDs they watch and the music they listen to. It may not seem overtly Christian, but it is incredibly educational! Form a panel of three which includes one leader and two children and allow them to view or listen to three DVDs/CDs for thirty seconds each. Then ask the panel whether they would they buy them or bin them and why. Periodically introduce Christian music. This teaches the children critical thought, which is very important for their development. Don't allow the children to get away with "because it's good" or "because I like it"; they must at least try and explain why. They need their attention drawn to the lyrics: ask if they know what the song is about.

Who Wants to be A Chocoholic?

Based on the TV game show *Who Wants to be a Millionaire?* a child is chosen from the audience. They are asked questions in increasing degrees of difficulty. They are given four answers to the questions and have to choose the right one. For a right answer they gain more chocolate, for a wrong answer they lose it all (you may want to consider using healthier options, such as fruit, or perhaps non-food related items such as stationery). The trick is to know when to quit and take the chocolate. The children have lifelines – though there are only two – they can ask the audience or ask a leader.

Aerobics workout

A piece of music is played and the children copy the leader at the front performing their aerobic workout.

Double dare

A child is chosen. The child then chooses a leader. The child is then given seven different envelopes, from which they must choose one. In each envelope there is a question – some easy, some very hard. The child will then make a decision before the envelope is open; will they answer the question or will the leader? The envelope is opened and the question is asked to whomever the child chose. If the child chose to answer the question but gets it wrong then s/he gets a shaving foam pie in the face. If she gets it right then s/he gets to place the pie in the leader's face. If the leader answers the question the same rules apply in reverse.

This slot can also be used for all sorts of fun items such as puppet skits, etc. Use it to have fun with the children.

> WARNING: There exists a group of people called the "What's the point of that?" people. They watch with cynical faces. The shake their heads and they ask "What's the point of that?" It's perfectly legitimate to have fun. But I find it best never to defend the fun items. It's best to smile and simply say "There's no point at all!" Watch the response.

Game 2 (5 minutes)

Make sure that different people are involved in Game 2 than were involved in Game 1.

Fun item 2 (5 minutes)

> COMMENT: All the items within the programme need to be joined together quite rapidly. The usual length of a session is just under two hours. Younger children may not cope with the full length of the programme. Condense the programme and introduce a simple craft time if you are working with children under seven years of age.

Bible Text (3 minutes)

We display the memory verse on the projector screen from the start of preaching time and refer to it frequently, but you may prefer to encourage the children to memorize the text. There are many ways to teach a Bible text, and a few ideas are highlighted, but there are literally hundreds. Be creative.

- Write the Bible text on balloons and burst the balloon as the verse is read.
- Make the verse into a jigsaw puzzle.
- Write the verse on an object which communicates its message, for example, "You are a light to my path" can be written on a lamp or in a drawing of a bulb.
- "The Lord is my shepherd" can be written on five cut-out sheep.

- Laminate the verse onto lots of tiny sheets of paper and give each child one to take home.

Remember that memorization of the verse is not as important as understanding. It may win them a prize being able to quote "The Lord is my shepherd", but it will change their lives if they understand it.

Announcements (2 minutes)

Summer camps, holiday clubs, colouring competitions, birthdays, special events, etc., all need mentioning here. If you are going to do birthdays then you must be consistent – don't do birthdays one week and then miss two weeks; some children will miss out and feel hurt.

Interview (5 minutes)

Invite one of the leaders, or one of the children, to tell the group what Jesus has done for them: how He's helped them in work/school, how He cares for them, how they first made their decision to become a Christian. If the person is very nervous, interview them. If they are more confident, allow them to speak freely – taking notice of the timing allowed for this section.

Preaching time

The rest of the programme falls under the heading "preaching time". This will include all worship, Bible lessons, illustrations and story. Take three minutes to explain the rules.

Inform the children that they are now moving into preaching time and this means everyone, still, silent and facing the front. There are some special rules, but if you are running the programme with a smaller group, they will not be needed.

- Anyone talking loses six points straight away without discussion. However, a leader will be walking around with tuck shop tokens or sweets and will place them in the hands of anyone who really deserves one.
- You must be excellently behaved to receive one; good is not enough – anyone can be good.
- You must keep facing the front. If you look at the leader

(who we refer to as a quiet seat watcher) they will not give you a token/sweet.
• If you get a sweet/token and play with it (or try and open it) then it will be taken off you.

Sweets and tokens are given sparingly. Maybe a sweet/token every three to four minutes. More than this moves the giving of sweets/tokens from an incentive to listen into a distraction.

Worship (10 minutes)

A quieter time of worship songs can be introduced. Encourage the children who know the words to close their eyes and begin to think about King Jesus. Take your time here: it is important to introduce them to worship.

Instruct the children that praise is generally loud and lively – a time where we have fun singing to God. Worship is where we come closer to God; think about God more. Worship comes from our hearts and our minds. It involves all our emotions. The definitions of praise and worship may be much broader and more theological than this, but a bite-size theological portion is more easily swallowed by an eight-year-old.

Blow the whistle at the end of worship and inform the children again that this is preaching time (the whistle can be put away now, it will no longer be needed).

Bible lesson (5 minutes)

There are various ideas to help with the presentation of the Bible lesson:
• Dress some of the children up as characters in the story.
• Use DVDs. The Recommended Resources section (Appendix 7) will give you some ideas.
• If you are presenting the story in narrative form then tell the story as Hollywood would – don't just read the account.

Illustrations 1–3 (5 minutes each)

Illustrations can take many forms.

Object lessons:

An object can be used to communicate a truth. For example:

Object needed: A light bulb and a sheet of paper

People are always complaining that we are wasting things. Turn off the light, you are wasting electricity; use the back of that piece of paper, don't waste paper. Don't leave the tap running, you are wasting water…

All these things are important and we mustn't waste things. But I heard a story once of someone who wasted something even more important. It was an old lady and she said one of the saddest things I have ever heard. She said that God had told her when she was young that she should be a missionary for Him and go to a far-away country. The old lady said that she hadn't gone because she had found something else to do and now she feels that she has wasted her life.

It's bad to waste money or electricity or paper or water. But it is the saddest thing in the world to waste a life. Being a Christian may be tough sometimes, but at least we will not waste our lives.

Video clips

With a video camera go to the streets and get a teenager to interview passers-by. Passers-by can be asked if they believe in God? If they own a Bible? What they understand by the word "trust"?

Commercial movie clips

Video clips can also be used to communicate various themes.

Testimonies: Personal testimony

Things which happen to us often illustrate important truths, here's an example:

I had to go on a journey once to a place in the north of the country. I got on a train very early in the morning and was on my way. We hadn't travelled very far when it started to snow. It kept on snowing and didn't look if it was ever going to stop snowing. When I was halfway there I had to change trains. When I got off my train the whole world had gone white. The snow kept on falling and most of the trains were cancelled. There were just a few trains left running; one was going back towards my home and another was going towards the direction I was heading but not exactly the right way.

I had to make a decision. It would have been the easiest thing in the world to get back on the other train and go home. But I didn't. I got on the other train. You see, I had friends waiting for me, and I didn't want to let them down. I got on the other train.

God is desperate for us to finish the journey we started with Him. He doesn't want us to turn back; He wants us to keep going.

The train took me to somewhere near where I wanted to go and then I had to get in a taxi for the last forty miles. The taxi couldn't get me all the way. So, in the freezing cold and well after midnight, I had to walk the last bit. And then to my horror I discovered the person I was going to stay with wasn't there. He hadn't been able to get home because of the snow. I had to phone someone else and only eventually found someone to stay with. But I had got there. I didn't turn back. I finished the journey. I reached the destination.

God didn't tell us it would be easy serving Him – in fact He promised that it would be hard at times. But we must keep going.

When we start something we need to see it through until the end.

Testimonies: Stories of others

Not only are stories about our own lives useful, things which happen to others can also be an excellent communication tool:

Once during the American War of Independence an accident happened as several of the American troops were travelling along a muddy path. A wagon they were using had overturned and was blocking the road. The captain of the troops lined up several of the men and was shouting at them to push and push and push to try and turn the wagon back over.

When the wagon wouldn't budge the captain got even more annoyed and shouted louder at his men to push. After some time a man on horseback arrived at the place where the wagon had turned over and asked: "Captain, why don't you help these men rather than just shout at them?"

But the captain was amazed at the request.

"I am their captain." he replied. "I should not dirty my uniform in such a manner."

With that the man got off his horse. His uniform was already dirty. He walked over to the men and said: "I will help! Let's push again."

Now with the help of this stranger the wagon was pushed upright.

The captain was glad that the wagon was restored but annoyed that this stranger should interfere. As the stranger got back onto his horse the captain demanded: "Who are you, sir? What gives you the right to interfere in my affairs?"

The man now on horseback smiled. "I am General George Washington and I interfere because you are in my army. And from now on, captain, you will lead by example."

The captain didn't know how to answer. So he simply said: "Yes, sir!"

That day the captain learned the importance of leading by example. Do we give a good example for others to follow or not?

Basically anything that will help to present the overall lesson can be placed here.

Story (15 minutes)

The story is the integral part of your communication – for help with presenting see the Communication section of this book. And note well, as I have mentioned before, do not try and explain the story or say, "This means, boys and girls…" The story will communicate in its own right. It's a good story!

Prayer/ministry (5 minutes)

Always ask for a response. Make an appeal. Ask the children who felt the lesson applied to them to stand. If it required forgiveness, pray a prayer of forgiveness together. Let the children respond by repeating the prayer after you. There should be a response. Sometimes you may need to give the children space to listen and encounter God themselves. Other times it may be important to lay a hand on their shoulder (ask permission from the child first) and pray for them. Each lesson gives you some suggestions, but be sensitive to the Holy Spirit and go for it.

Next week (3 minutes)

Highlight next week's programme. Keep it exciting: "Next week everyone who comes will get a creme egg"; "Next week we'll hear the concluding part of this exciting story", etc.

The Extra Stuff – Appendix

Sample Letter for Schools

Our Church * Our Town * Our Area

Wednesday, 14 June 2017

Dear Head teacher/Assembly Co-ordinator,

Re: Assemblies for Primary Schools

The last academic year was interesting to say the least. We have taken nearly 100 assemblies a term, taken several harvest presentations to parents, several carol concerts for parents and old folk and a number of those ever-interesting OFSTED assemblies – we now have over 20 OFSTED assemblies completed. So, here is the first assembly series of the new academic year:

January – Because He Tried
People thought it was impossible to run a four-minute mile until Roger Banister did it, then many others ran under four minutes. People thought Everest couldn't be climbed until Edmund Hilary climbed it – then many others climbed it. Sometimes when we think something is impossible we never actually try. The mountain's too big, the distance too great... Sometimes when we try we discover that things open up in front of us, just because we tried. This is the story of George and his determination to become a lawyer even though he and his family have never left the farm.

February – Green Noses
A return to Max Lucado's "Punchinello" stories – you may remember the first story, "You are Special" – if not this isn't a problem; the stories are stand-alones.

The Wemmicks have all started painting their noses green so that they can be like the other Wemmicks. Individuality is the main theme of this assembly.

March – Three Trees
This assembly has been used in many places by many different people, but it is still very popular. One day a farmer plants three very special seeds. Three trees grow tall and strong. Every day they discuss what they want to be when they are eventually chopped down. They all have big ambitions. But the fulfilment of those ambitions is beyond their wildest dreams. The Easter story is woven into this assembly.

Booking assemblies for the next three months is a simple process of picking up the phone between 9 a.m. and 12 noon each day and working out three suitable dates with our administrator. If you are part of a combined school I can visit twice or we can do back-to-back assemblies, the choice is yours. There is no charge for this service; it is very much a part of our vision to be a positive part of our community. I will also endeavour over the next couple of months to visit each of the schools within the parish to see if we can be of further service as a church.

Yours faithfully

Mark Griffiths

Five Year Planner

	Year 1	Year 2	Year 3	Year 4	Year 5
October					
November					
December					
CHRISTMAS					
January					
February					
March					
EASTER					
June					
July					

Develop one assembly each month to be repeated in all the schools you visit that month. At the end of the month write the assembly up. After five years you will have enough assemblies to continue to repeat assemblies on a five-year rotation.

Sample Leaflet

FRANTIC
THE CHILDREN'S EVENT FOR 5-11S

Bouncy Castle ✦ Multimedia
Face Painting ✦ Computer Games
Competitions ✦ Dance ✦ Live Music
Fun Quizzes ✦ Puppets ✦
Table Top Football ✦ Team Games ✦
Stories ✦ Cafe Area ✦ Quizzes ✦ Videos ✦
Basketball ✦ Much More

ADMISSION ONLY £1

FURTHER INFORMATION ON (01908)

Children's Club Colouring Competition

My Children's Club Colouring Competition

To be returned on Friday evening at the start of children's club.

Name: _____

The best colouring will win a prize!

Lesson Format Template

	Programme	Item
Section 1	Welcome	
	Rules	
	Prayer	
	Introductory praise	
	Game 1	
	Praise	
	Fun item 1	
	Game 2	
	Fun item 2	
	Bible text	
	Announcements	
	Interview	
	Worship time	
Section 2	Bible lesson	
Preaching	Illustration 1	
Time	Illustration 2	
	Illustration 3	
	Story	
	Prayer	

Sample Lesson from *Impact* by Mark Griffiths

Beginnings

	Programme	Item
Section 1	Welcome	
	Rules	
	Prayer	
	Praise	
	Game 1	Lego 1 – Order out of chaos
	Praise (x2)	
	Fun item 1	
	Game 2	Lego 2 – Towers
	Fun Item 2	
	Bible text	Genesis 1:2
	Announcements	
	Interview	
	Worship (x2)	
Section 2	**Bible lesson**	Genesis 1
Preaching	**Illustration 1**	*Toy Story 2*
Time	**Illustration 2**	Formless and empty
	Story	Carlos (1)
	Prayer	

Overview

It started with God bringing order out of chaos, creating a world of perfection. But God has a flair for the dramatic, and Genesis 1:2 is the build-up before the explosion. The world was empty and dark, with the Spirit of God hovering. Something was bound to happen – God was there. And the same God hovers over the lives of children, waiting to explode.

Games

Game 1

LEGO 1 – ORDER OUT OF CHAOS

PREPARATION: A pile of Lego for each team, placed at B.

PLAYERS: Four players per team.

SET-UP: Players stand at A.

OBJECT: The players run from A to B, create "something" out of the chaotic pieces of Lego within two minutes and then bring their creation back to A.

WINNING: The team with the best construction wins.

Game 2

LEGO 2 – TOWERS

PREPARATION: As for Game 1.

PLAYERS: Four players per team.

SET-UP: The Lego pieces are placed at B.

OBJECT: The first person races from A to B, collects a piece of Lego (only one piece) and returns. This continues until all the pieces are collected. While the pieces are being collected someone at A attempts to construct the tallest free-standing construction with the pieces.

WINNING: The tallest free-standing construction wins. Remember: free-standing – the towers must not be held.

Preaching Time

Bible Lesson

GENESIS 1:1 – 2:4

> "The earth was formless and empty, darkness was over the surface of the deep, and the Spirit of God was hovering over the waters." (Genesis 1:2, NIV)

Genesis is the very first book in the Bible, and it's where we will be spending most of our time for the next couple of weeks. It has some great accounts of Noah and his ark, of Abraham and Isaac, and of Joseph and his coat of many colours. All these are found in Genesis. But right at the start of Genesis is a very special account indeed. It is the story of creation – of how it all began. It tells of how God created day and night and animals and plants and flowers. Listen as I read you the first verses from the first book in the Bible:

In the beginning God created the heavens and the earth. The earth was barren, with no form of life; it was under a roaring ocean covered with darkness. But the Spirit of God was moving over the water. God said, "I command light to shine!" And light started shining. God looked at the light and saw that it was good. He separated light from darkness and named the light "Day" and the darkness "Night". Evening came and then morning – that was the first day.

God said, "I command a dome to separate the water above it from the water below it." And that's what happened. God made the dome and named it "Sky". Evening came and then morning – that was the second day.

God said, "I command the water under the sky to come together in one place, so there will be dry ground." And that's what happened. God named the dry ground "Land", and he named the water "Ocean". God looked at what he had done and saw that it was good. God said, "I command the earth to produce all kinds of plants, including fruit trees and grain." And that's what happened. The earth produced all kinds of vegetation. God looked at what he had done, and it was good. Evening came and then morning – that was the third day.

God said, "I command lights to appear in the sky and to separate day from night and to show the time for seasons, special days, and years. I command them to shine on the earth." And that's what happened. God made two powerful lights, the brighter one to rule the day and the other to rule the night. He also made the stars. Then God put these lights in the sky to shine on the earth, to rule day and night, and to separate light from darkness. God looked at what he had done, and it was good. Evening came and then morning – that was the fourth day.

God said, "I command the ocean to be full of living creatures, and I command birds to fly above the earth." So God made the giant sea monsters and all the living creatures that swim in the ocean. He also made every kind of bird. God looked at what he had done, and it was good. Then he gave the living creatures his blessing – he told the ocean creatures to live everywhere in the ocean and the birds to live everywhere on earth. Evening came and then morning – that was the fifth day.

God said, "I command the earth to give life to all kinds of tame animals, wild animals, and reptiles." And that's what happened. God made every one of them. Then he looked at what he had done, and it was good.

God said, "Now we will make humans, and they will be like us. We will let them rule the fish, the birds, and all other living creatures."

So God created humans to be like himself; he made men and women. God gave them his blessing and said: "Have a lot of children! Fill the earth with people and bring it under your control. Rule over the fish in the ocean, the birds in the sky, and every animal on the earth. I have provided all kinds of fruit and grain for you to eat. And I have given the green plants as food for everything else that breathes. These will be food for animals, both wild and tame, and for birds." God looked at what he had done. All of it was very good! Evening came and then morning – that was the sixth day.

So the heavens and the earth and everything else were created.

By the seventh day God had finished his work, and so he rested. God blessed the seventh day and made it special because on that day he rested from his work. That's how God created the heavens and the earth.

Illustration 1

Toy Story 2

Object needed: A video clip.

Play the introductory scenes from *Toy Story 2* – you'll know which part to play and where to stop from the narrative that works with it below.

That was a small clip from *Toy Story 2*. It is before all the action really gets going and before Woody's adventure really begins. It shows just a quiet, ordinary bedroom. Some of you may live quiet, ordinary lives; maybe the action hasn't got going yet. But for those who will let God be part of their lives, the adventure is yet to begin.

Illustration 2

Formless and empty

Objects needed: Modelling clay, Flash paper, matches.

The whole story of creation is wonderful, but I particularly like the first part: "The earth was formless and empty, darkness was over the surface of the deep, and the Spirit of God was hovering."

"The world was formless and empty." Let's use our imaginations. Imagine "formless and empty". That would be like this modelling clay: no shape, no form, of no real use. How about, "darkness was over the surface of the deep"? (*Turn the lights off and ask for complete silence.*)

Then the Spirit of God was hovering. (*Light a match.*)

You see, when the Spirit of God is hovering, you can be pretty sure that something is going to happen. And the Spirit of God is hovering over your lives tonight, lives that may seem to have no shape or form, lives which are dark because of that stuff called sin – the junk, garbage, rubbish in our lives. But God's hovering. He's about to do something. He wants to do something.

And the Spirit of God hovered over the formless and empty earth and then God said, "Let there be light." (*Light the flash paper.*) And there was light. (*Put the lights back on.*)

God wants to take your life, which you may feel is empty and a bit formless, and make it into something remarkable.

So in a way, we are like modelling clay. It is formless; it has no real shape, like many of our lives. But it is God who puts the shape and form into us. He gives us purpose – we use a big word: destiny. This means becoming what God wants us to become.

STORY – Carlos (1)

Carlos sat down in his bedroom and looked around the sea of beds in the dormitory. There were fifteen beds in all. It was crowded, but comfortable. All the boys who shared the dormitory had their own cupboard for storing their things – not that Carlos had many things. He had two pairs of trousers that had been given to him, two T-shirts, a jumper and a sprinkling of underwear and socks. Oh, and the coat that one of the older boys had kindly given him because it didn't fit him any longer.

Carlos looked into the mirror fastened to his cupboard. He stared. Two bright blue eyes stared back. He began to dress for bed. He put on his boxer shorts and looked at himself in the mirror one more time. He was hoping that his muscles would arrive soon, but there didn't seem to be any signs yet. He flexed his right arm, but there really was nothing there – nothing, that is, except Carlos' strange mark. On the top of his left arm there was a very curious shape. It looked like a wave splashing into the air. Carlos often wondered what it was, but recently had decided it was just a birthmark. Carlos crawled into bed and lay back on his pillow; he pushed his long, curly blond hair out of his eyes and stared up at the ceiling. Carlos was nine years old. The place he lived in was not his real home, but it felt like home to him. He grabbed his stuffed rabbit, which by now was looking a bit the worse for wear, snuggled it under his chin and began to drop off to sleep.

Carlos' earliest memories were very happy ones. He remembered being rocked to sleep by his father, and the feel of the cot blankets on his face. His fondest memories were of looking up into his mother's radiant blue eyes as she sang to him a song about cows jumping over moons, and plates running away with spoons.

The little stuffed rabbit was his only reminder of that time now. Somehow that world had vanished away from him, and now he lived with many other boys and girls in an orphanage run by monks. Carlos lay on his bed thinking, little realizing that everything was about to change.

(To be continued...)

Recommended Resources

This list is in no particular order and is undoubtedly not comprehensive, but it does represent the collected wisdom of dozens and dozens of children and family workers who responded to my Facebook requests for resource recommendations. This is their list:

Wisdom and inspirational books

- *One Generation from Extinction* – Mark Griffiths
- *Whose Child is This?* – Bill Wilson
- *The Josiah Generation* – Olly Goldenberg
- *Children, Can You Hear Me?* – Brad Jersak
- *Honey, I Blew Up the Kid's Ministry* – Andrew Shepherd
- *Children's Ministry Leadership* – Jim Wideman
- *The Spiritual Guidance of Children* – Jerome W. Berryman
- *God's Generals for Kids* – Roberts Liardon and Olly Goldenberg (many editions now available)
- *Slugs and Snails and Puppy Dogs' Tails: Helping Boys Connect with God* – Carolyn Edwards
- *Mend the Gap: Can the Church Reconnect the Generations?* – Jason Gardner
- *Formational Children's Ministry* – Ivy Beckwith
- *Raising Children in a Digital Age* – Bex Lewis
- *Through the Eyes of a Child* – Anne Richards and Peter Privett
- *Children's Ministry in the Way of Jesus* – David Csinos and Ivy Beckwith
- *The Child in Christian Thought and Practice* – Marcia Bunge
- *The Child in the Bible* – Marcia Bunge (ed.)
- *Children and the Theologians* – Jerome W. Berryman
- *Side by side with God in Everyday Life* – Yvonne Morris
- *Exploring God's love in Everyday Life* – Yvonne Morris
- *Will our Children have Faith?* – John H. Westerhoff
- *Blended* – Eleanor Bird

General resource

- *Godly Play* (and associated books) – Jerome W. Berryman
- *Messy Church* (and associated books) – Lucy Moore
- *And For Your Children* – John and Chris Leech
- www.Max7.org

Family-specific

- *Think Orange* – Reggie Joiner
- *Children, Families and God* – Lynn Alexander
- *Loving Our Kids on Purpose* – Danny Silk
- *Getting Your Kids Through Church* – Rob Parsons and Katharine Hill (Care for the Family)
- *Parentalk: The Primary Years* – Rob Parsons and Katharine Hill (Care for the Family)
- *Together with God* – Ed Mackenzie and Gareth Crispin
- *Children in the Bible* – Anne Richards
- *Prayer-Saturated Kids* – Cheryl Sacks and Arlywn Lawrence
- *Six Sacred Rules of Family* – Tim and Sue Muldoon
- *Collide* – Tammy Tolman
- *Sticky Faith* – Fuller Youth Institute
- *Comfort in the Darkness* – Rachel Turner
- *Parenting Children for a Life of Faith* – Rachel Turner
- *Parenting Children for a Life of Confidence* – Rachel Turner
- *Parenting Children for a Life of Purpose* – Rachel Turner
- *The Growth of Love* – Child Development – Keith J. White

Kids' devotionals

- *Jesus Calling: 365 Devotions for Kids* – Sarah Young

To help families

- www.godventures.com – books and resources
- Treasure Boxes from The Treasure Box People
- *Play Through the Bible* – Alice Buckley
- *Bake Through the Bible* – Alice Buckley
- *The Power of a Praying Parent* – Stormie Omartian
- *At Home with God* – Olly Goldenberg

- *The Family Devotional, from Engage Worship* – Sam and Sara Hargreaves
- *Beginning with God* – Alison Mitchell
- www.familyministry.co.uk
- *All Together* – Family devotions – Steve and Bekah Legg

Children and spiritual gifts

- *Children and the Holy Spirit* – John and Chris Leach
- *Reclaiming a Generation: Ishamel* (the book formerly known as *Angels with Dirty Faces* may be tricky to find, but I think it would be against the children's ministry law not to include it!)

Prayer

- *The Spy Kit* – A prayer resource – Olly and Helen Goldenberg

Curriculum

Lightbringers with Freedom in Christ – Mark Griffiths and Jo Foster (due for publication May 2018)

Fusion – Mark Griffiths

Impact – Mark Griffiths

Detonate – Mark Griffiths

Excavate for pre-schoolers – Anna Martin

Excavate for 5–7s – Anna Martin

Excavate for 8–11s – Anna Martin

Discovery Club – David Goodwin www.kidsreach.org.au

Roots – Scripture Union

Light – Scripture Union

Living Stones – Susan Sayers

Identity – Matt Schwarzenberger

Connected – Elaine Webster

Explore Together – Scripture Union

Transformation Station – Bill Wilson (Metro World Child)

Changing the Future, One Life at a Time – Urban Saints

7 Gifts for our Children – Daron Pratt – http://nnsw.adventist.org.au/family

Give Me 5: 700+ great ideas – Olly Goldenberg

Sunday-based curriculum and other web resources with web links

www.rootsontheweb.com Roots

www.scriptureunion.org.uk/light/ Light

www.kevinmayhew.com Living Stones

www.handinhandconference.com/ Children's ministry

www.goteach.org.uk Bible teaching material

www.urbansaints.org Changing the future one life at a time

www.thebiblecurriculum.com Bible through storytelling, crafts and games

www.spiritseasons.com Sunday school curriculum

www.barnabasinchurches.org.uk Resources for children's and families' ministry

www.web.energize.net Web-based resources

www.bigministries.co.uk For 7–11s

www.kidsuk.org Charity that links with churches and schools

www.FamilyFriendlyChurches.org.uk Ideas and resources for children's ministry

www.resoundworship.org Song-writing collective

www.childrenssociety.org.uk/church

www.theworshipwell.org Worship resources

www.vineyardchurches.org.uk/equipping-the-churches/kids/ Materials for children's ministry

CDs

(Massive thanks to Nigel Hemming for providing much of this section, although I had to add his own CDs because although they are fabulous, Nigel is a humble chap!)

- *Carry the Light* – New Wine Kids
- *Mission Unstoppable* – Olly Goldenberg
- *I Belong* – Tammy Tolman
- *Be Like You* – Tammy Tolman
- *Arise* – Brendon and Cathy Clancy
- *Praise Party 1* – Andy Piercy
- *Little Songs for Little Children* – Ishmael
- *God is Great* – Colin Buchanan
- *Shout Praises!* Kids Gospel
- *Sing me to Sleep* – Jodie Jones
- *Big Family of God* – Nick and Becky Drake
- *Flabbergasted* – Doug Horley
- *Oomph, Chuffed, Whoopah Wahey* – and anything else by Doug Horley
- *God You're So Cool* – Simon Parry
- *Welcome to the Big Academy* – Big Ministries
- *This is Love* – Jim Bailey
- *Stand Together* (primary school) New Wine Kids' albums
- Hillsong Kids' albums: *Follow you, Supernatural, Super Strong God*, and more…
- *Come Alive* – Bethel Kids
- *Unique* – Nicky and Becky Drake
- *Great Big God* (many volumes) – Nigel Hemming and Vineyard Kids
- *All of My Days* – Citikidz (with action DVD and backing tracks)
- *Saturate* – Citikidz (with action DVD and backing tracks)

CDs for younger children and parents/carers

- *Mr Cow* – Julia Plaut
- *Tots Praise* – Children's ministry
- *Get Up and Dance* – Early years
- *I Love Jesus* – Olly and Helen Goldenberg

Children's fiction

- *Children of the Voice* – Ishmael (maybe hard to find, but I love this series)
- *Hanging on Every Word* – Mark Griffiths
- *The Lion Storyteller Bible* – Bob Hartman
- *The Lion Storyteller Awesome Book of Stories* – Bob Hartman
- Pretty much anything else by Bob Hartman

Children as leaders and peer-led small groups

- David Club – Andrew Shepherd
- Big Cell – Andy and Catherine Kennedy

DVDs

- *Jewish Feasts: An Introduction for Children* – Olly Goldenberg
- *Jewish Insights: Lessons from the Old Testament* – Olly Goldenberg

Facebook

- New Wine Kids
- Kids' Leaders' Network

Websites

- www.new-wine.org
- www.stickyfaith.org
- www.childrencan.co.uk

Software/games

- Guardians of Ancora – SU app (free download)
- www.theaetherlight.com
- "God for Kids" app

For pregnant mothers and newborns

- CD – *Jesus, Your Baby and You: Resting in God's Presence During Your Pregnancy* – compiled by Olly and Helen Goldenberg
- CD – *Sleep Sound in Jesus* – Michael Card

- Book – *Supernatural Childbirth* – Jackie Mize
- Book – *Jesus, Your Baby, and You* – Helen and Olly Goldenberg

Blogs

www.markgriffiths.net – Leadership development, mission, children and families

http://tammytolman.blogspot.co.uk/ – Leadership development, families

www.belleministry.com/ – Especially for girls to discover value and identity

www.childrencan.co.uk/blog/ – Leadership, children, spiritual gifts, mission and evangelism

www.theresource.org.uk/blog-posts – Leadership development and resources for children and family workers – and so much more

http://jimwideman.com/blog-2/ – Children's ministry expert

http://flamecreativekids.blogspot.co.uk/ – Creative children's ministry